207 Ways To Market Your Childcare Business
AND GET MORE ENQUIRIES THROUGH YOUR DOOR

Nick Williams

207 Ways To Market Your Childcare Business

And Get More Enquiries Through Your Door

First published in Great Britain in 2017 by Nick Williams via Type & Tell

Copyright © 2017 Nick Williams

A CIP catalogue record for this book is available from the British Library

ISBN 978-1-78745-051-6

Head on over to our Facebook Group

www.facebook.com/groups/ChildcareBusinessGrowth
to connect with other amazing childcare
professionals around the World.

www.childcarebusinessgrowth.com

Acknowledgments

I'd like to thank all the amazing childcare professionals that have kindly allowed me to include examples of their great work within this book. You are an inspiration to us all.

I'd like to thank everyone that has kindly provided a testimonial for the book. Your constructive feedback has been a big help throughout this whole process.

Finally, I'd like to say a huge thank you to all my clients. I love waking up every day and working with you towards your dreams. They say that when you love what you do it shouldn't feel like work and I can honestly say that is the case working alongside you. Some of you have already gone through huge transformations in your business and I want to thank you for believing in me to help you achieve your dream.

This book is dedicated to my wife, my children and my parents. Without your help, encouragement and love this book wouldn't have been possible.

Foreword

Mention the word Marketing to many small business owners and you can see them visibly shudder at the mere thought of it. Whilst many appreciate the necessity of it, they lack enthusiasm and certainly time to be able to put together a whole strategy that will work to support their business. What does it really mean, what do I have to do and how much will it cost me in time and money are just some of the questions they come up with.

Enter Nick Williams. I met Nick just a few months ago and was immediately enthused by his great ambition to dispel the myths about marketing and to get the early years world better focused on both marketing and customer service. Nick has the ability to inspire everyone to do and be more, and for those of us who struggle for time then Nick even has the solution – he can do it for you!

So, who better than to write a book on the subject than Nick, and what a great book it is. The key concepts and ideas that Nick shares here are well worth reading. Even if you are a seasoned marketer, there will certainly be an idea or two to spark a new campaign or initiative in your business. Take notes and take action. Good Luck!

Tricia Wellings
Director & Founder
Foundation Focus & MBK Training

Introduction

First of all, I just want to congratulate you on choosing to work in such a great industry and being brave enough to open your own business. But because you did, you are helping parents in a huge way by providing a safe, caring and nurturing environment for their child to grow into confident, clever children; whilst dealing with all the stresses and strains that running your own business can bring. So again, I just want to congratulate you and tell you well done for doing such a great job.

It's hard running any business, particularly in the childcare sector when a huge amount of your time is not only taken up looking after the children and liaising with parents, but also dealing with endless amounts of paperwork and if you've got staff, you've also got the job of keeping them motivated.

With all your other priorities, marketing is often neglected in our sector; but our customers can typically spend anywhere from £3,000 to £30,000 per year using our services. So, they could end up spending up to £90,000 over a three-year period. That's an awful lot of money, but we spend hardly any time marketing our services to those parents to get them to enrol in the first place and then build on that relationship when they do become a customer. It's what I call childcare relationship marketing. So, what does that mean; well it's not just about marketing your business to get in a new enquiry, it's then continuing to market and nurture your relationship when they are a customer.

I wrote this book to share ideas that I've implemented in our businesses and with my clients in the hope that it will encourage you to do the same. The majority of the concepts in here are easy to implement and can be done very quickly. You can either read it page by page, or jump to a section that you've already started work on. This book isn't a guarantee of success though; nothing will happen unless you implement these concepts fully into your business and make marketing a key priority for your growth and success.

The concepts within this book are the key to supercharging your marketing efforts in a very short period of time, but nothing can ever replace a network of peer group support and accountability. That's why you should head to **www.childcarebusinessgrowth.com** and continue your journey with us directly. You'll discover lots of free content, resources, podcasts and the opportunity to grow faster with our coaching and mentorship programs.

I hope you enjoy the book.

Contents

Fundamentals

Introduction

Before we get into the core tactics within the book, I just wanted to cover off some fundamentals that I wish I had put in place when I started my first business. These fundamentals will help you create a solid foundation to start your marketing, so I'd highly recommend putting them in place before you start to spend any money on marketing your business.

Know your ideal customer

I'm not just talking about knowing that they are parents or parents to be. You need to define the gender, age bracket, background, job, things they like, things they dislike, why they come to you over another setting. Once you know your ideal customer, you can market to them accordingly.

Here's an example of our ideal customer (we refer to this as our customer Avatar) - Mary is 32 with 3 children aged 6, 3 and 1. She loves her children dearly, but is also very career driven and Dad is away a lot, so she doesn't get a lot of support. Mary requires care 4 days a week and then has Friday at home to collect the children and spend time with her youngest two children. Mary chose our nursery because she loves the family approach and the location was perfect. She loves daily progress from her children's key workers and appreciates the gifts that we send out to her for birthdays. She always joins in our posts on Facebook and always enters competitions.

Elevator Pitch

Imagine if you entered a lift with a parent who was clearly stressed and was on the phone trying to arrange childcare. You've got 15 seconds before they get out of the lift to explain what you do and why they should come to you.

So, here's a simple template to use to create your elevator pitch. We help (insert ideal client) to (overcome common problem) in (time frame).

For example. "We help parents by providing high-quality childcare to children aged __ to __. We stand out from the competition as we're family run, we send you daily updates and photos of your child throughout the day and we have the largest outdoor space in _____. Would you like to arrange a tour to show you how we can help you?" So, every time you meet someone from now on, you have a perfect pitch to describe how your service can help them.

Solve Their Problems

People are usually looking for a solution to a problem and in this case it is the best childcare for their child. However, there are lots of other problems that parents have prior to choosing their childcare. Potty training, or sleep times are just a few problems parents want a solution to. Therefore, providing lots of useful content to assist with these problems will help parents build a relationship with you and start to know, like and trust you. You can do this via useful guides, blog posts, or even videos.

Check your enquiry process

It's so important to make sure all your forms of enquiry are working correctly. Are telephone enquiries getting to you, are web forms working, are emails being responded to. Web links can break, message pads can be lost. Test them regularly to make sure the process is running smoothly.

Give them the WWWWWHC

When advertising your services in any format, it is important to remember to include all of the following:
1. Who it's ideal for?
2. Why it's beneficial for them?
3. What is involved?
4. Where it's located?
5. When it takes place or is available?
6. How they can take part?
7. Call to action

Provide real value

This can start to happen well before they become a customer. You can provide them with advice and guidance on other child development topics, or help on looking for activities to do with their child. Then when they start at your setting, always try and exceed their expectations with the service you provide. Raise your hand as high as you can to deliver outstanding service.

Google Maps

Make sure your business is officially listed on Google My Business by going to **www.google.com/business**. Once you've secured your business make sure that all the relevant data is up-to-date and you keep adding photos and encourage parents to review your business.

Assess your follow up process

It's so important to always check your follow up process. If you're using an automation service, are the tasks scheduling correctly and are you and your team completing those tasks in a timely manner. Are you continuing to follow up weeks later if the prospect still hasn't made a decision? It's important to keep providing value and testimonials to those prospects until they either decide to buy, or tell you they're not interested anymore.

Calls to Action

Every piece of marketing you put out, including social media posts should have some form of call to action - what to do next, download the guide, like the page, request a tour. Take a look through all of your marketing material and make sure you have a clear Call to Action.

First Impressions Count

Research shows that we only have seven seconds to make a good first impression. So a nice big smile with a firm handshake and a professional appearance are key. Remember, first impressions apply to any type of contact they have with your business. That might be your website,

Facebook page, or a member of your team. Take the time to review each one of these and ask the question - Is that a good first impression of my business?

Professional looking website

Having a professional looking website is key for me. It doesn't need to be flash, but it needs to have all the following included:
1. A clear description of you and your services
2. A nice and simple web address
3. Clear links to other pages
4. All your contact details (including social media links)
5. Photos of you and your setting
6. Testimonials
7. Clear call to action
8. Work on desktop and mobile
9. Up-to-date fresh quality content
10. Have the basic SEO information

Now most websites have this basic information, but miss the call to action. So, an example of this would be - 'Check Availability, Download Our Free Checklist'.

I talk about this more later in lead magnets, but you are giving a clear call to action and asking them for their contact details in exchange for some type of information they want to know.

Here's a great example of a nursery using our template. We haven't even scrolled down the page and it has all the things we pointed out in the list above, including a video and three calls to action - Apply now, book a visit, or request a parent pack.

If you'd like a professional website design that has everything listed above head over to www.childcarebusinessgrowth.com.

Speed of response

My personal opinion on this is the quicker you can get on to an enquiry the better. If someone asks for a parent pack, we try our very best to drop it at their home the very same day. Why, because no one else is going to take the time to do that. It's easy; we have the packs prepared and drop them off on our way home from the setting. Now, this wasn't planned when we first created our packs, but some letter boxes are much smaller than others, so sometimes our pack doesn't go through the door. This has massively worked in our favour, because we often end up having to ring the doorbell to hand deliver it to them. Parents are so impressed by this and often end up having a 10-15 minute chat on their door, which is an environment that they are familiar with, so they feel in control and usually tend to ask lots of questions. We get parents asking to book a viewing there and then, or 80% of the time they call us the next day to book.

We've had parents secure places before they've even seen the setting just based on this experience. This doesn't just apply to parent packs, it applies to any time a prospect gets in contact; the quicker you respond the better.

Map it Out

It's important to map out exactly where your customers come from. That way you'll know whether you are focusing your marketing efforts in the right area. The best way to do this is to purchase a custom map online and put your location right in the centre of it. Then map out where your existing parents come from. You might find that there are particular areas where the majority of your existing parents come from, so it would be worthwhile making a more targeted effort in those areas and sharing in your message that lots of your children already come from the area.

Other things to map out would be new housing developments, commercial areas and where your competition are located. Use different colours for each reference. Doing this will not only give you a much better understanding of your geographical spread, but will highlight potential areas that you aren't really targeting. This is an example of a map where the setting is in the centre, allowing us to map out a radius around the setting. I would personally recommend getting a map with a scale of 1: 50,000 - that way you cover a bigger area and can still see exactly which post code / zip code the parent is coming from.

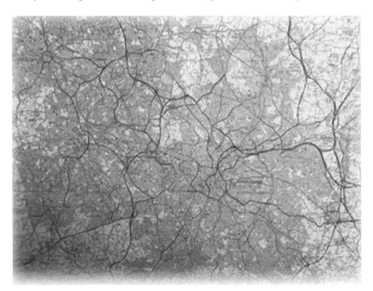

PMMFS

We all want to be made to feel special and appreciated every now and again, so imagine if everyone was walking around with a post it note on their head saying PMMFS - Please Make Me Feel Special.

Even if we're having a terrible day, we should always look for something positive to say when greeting another person. It helps build rapport and likeability.

Tracking your competition

It's so important to keep an eye on what your competition are doing. I'm not saying that you should copy them in anyway, but they maybe offering something that you hadn't thought of, or they may have a USP (unique selling proposition). What information are they sharing on social media, have they changed their prices. If you know what your competition are doing, that way you can be better prepared when a prospect aks you how you compare to the competition. You'll also find that there are some settings near you that are doing better than others, so it's important to know why. A great place to start is by liking their Facebook page and signing up to any newsletters or downloads that they have. Of course, you also want to ring them and get an idea of their pricing and availability. If your competition is a very large setting, then you may be able to find some of their example adverts on a tool called Similar Web, or Spyfu. These two tools allow you to type in the web addresses of your larger competitors and it gives you examples (and others) take a look at what the competition is doing. It shows you examples of which adverts are doing well and where they are getting their website traffic from. If you'd like to get your hands on our FREE competition tracker worksheet, just head on over to www.childcaremarketingideas.com/competitorsheet, submit your email and we'll send it straight over to you.

Make Time to Market

Marketing is often something that doesn't receive enough attention in childcare businesses. Your setting may already be full, but that doesn't mean you should stop marketing your business as you need to keep your pipeline full of prospects for the future. It's far easier to maintain your marketing than letting it slack off and having to start all over again. Make sure you allocate time during your week appropriately. So, if you're over 80% full you won't need to allocate as much time as someone who is only 50% full.

Understand your market

Your setting might be in a very deprived area, or you could be located in a very affluent area. You might be surrounded by large businesses or in a heavily populated residential area. It's so important to understand the demographics of your area so you can adjust your strategy and marketing accordingly. My message to a heavily populated residential area would be completely different to if my business was surrounded by large businesses. So my message would be more traditional for the residential areas, whereas for the businesses I'd be focussing on arranging corporate memberships and talking about the ease of dropping and collecting your child before and after work.

FAQs

Most enquiries tend to ask the same questions, so when someone asks a new question, take the time to write down your best possible answer. Then take the time to learn those answers. That way you and your team will always be confident that you're all delivering the same high quality answer.

Quick rebrand

Childcare marketing is still significantly behind most other industries with it's sophistication and if you haven't updated your brand in a while, a mini makeover could make the World of difference. A more modern font, bright colours and a strong current message that appeals to your exact audience can make a significant difference.

Feedback from non joiners

Ok, so your setting isn't going to appeal to everyone, but it's so important to get feedback from people who didn't join your setting. It could be the price, the location, anything. You won't know unless you ask. One of the best times to do this is immediately after they have been for a viewing, send them out a link to a short survey.

Create a marketing plan & calendar

We all get caught up in the day to day running of our business and can sometimes forget about marketing our businesses until it's almost too late. Planning ahead is crucial. It allows you to plan for peak enquiry times and make sure your campaigns are in place. You can plan your marketing accordingly based on events happening throughout the year, like holiday periods, or seasonal change. It's a great way to test different promotions throughout the year. You then want to breakdown your calendar into Prospects and Existing Parents. You may run a promotional offer for new prospects, while you're running a referral program for your existing parents. Then you can look at splitting your marketing activity down into two further categories - Evergreen and Monthly promotions. Evergreen is activity that you consistently do on a monthly basis; whereas monthly campaigns tie into the holidays during that period.

Tracking your ROI

Tracking your Return on Investment (ROI) means are you tracking where your enquiries are coming from and which marketing campaigns got them to enquire. For example, you might get an enquiry from a search on Google, or another enquiry from a local mother and baby group. If you're not asking the enquiry how they heard about you, then you've no idea which of your marketing efforts are working, so you could be wasting money. Every time a new enquiry comes in you should be tracking it on some form of spreadsheet. A way to do this is to create a simple table like the image below and log each enquiry against the source that it came from.

Once you know where your enquiries are coming from you can then work out what it cost to get that enquiry. For example, if you spent £100 on Facebook ads in the month and you got ten new enquiries from Facebook, and one of them enrolled in your program. Let's say the value of that enrolment was worth £5,000 for the year, that would mean you generated £5,000 from £100 in ad spend, giving you a 500% return on investment. Now if that enrolment stays with you for another three years, that would mean you've got a 1,500% return on investment! That's huge, all from a £100 ad spend on Facebook. Now you know you've got a great return from that marketing source, you can now see that it's easily worth putting more money into Facebook ads. Tracking is vital to know where to spend your money.

	January	February	March	April	May	June
Free Checklist						
Check Availability						
Book A Showaround						
Free Funded Place						
Facebook Call						
Google Call						
Just Showed Up						
Holiday Care						
Day Nurseries						
No. of new leads						

I've included a simple example of a tracking sheet here. All you do is put the lead source down the left and the month along the top. You can then track which of these leads converted into paying customers. You can just keep adding to this as you get a new lead source.

Tracking Phone Numbers

Tracking numbers allow you to set up a designated phone line for each piece of marketing you have. That way you can track exactly the number of phone calls you have received and which marketing is working best for you. You can also keep track of how many calls you missed and what times those calls were coming in. That way you can hold your team accountable. The majority of companies offering this service provide you with the opportunity to listen to all the calls, so you can find out exactly what questions parents are asking and then create the best possible response to those questions. It's not only a great way to track what marketing works, it's a great way to help train your team and improve your telephone skills.

Build Your List

I always use this scenario to help people get an understanding of how important lists are and where they should be stored. Just imagine all your files went up on fire and you had no records of enquiries or your existing parents. Storing lists online in a CRM (Customer Relationship Management) system is crucial. That way if anything was to ever go wrong with paper-based copies you have everything stored online. The next thing is to segment your list into various groups. For example, current existing parents, past parents, current enquiries, past enquiries that didn't sign up, people interested in holiday programs, people who have downloaded free guides or reports. The more you segment your list, the more you can tailor your message to speak to that exact person. You may want to send out a referral campaign to existing and past parents, but the message you would use to engage them would need to be different. Another way to segment your lists are birthdays, or year they started with your setting.

We use a great CRM system for all of our lists that's easy to use and priced accordingly to your budget. You can find out more by visiting: **http://bit.ly/CMI-Active-Campaign**

Be found on the Map

It's so important to make sure you are listed on the main search engines like Google, Bing and Yahoo, so start by searching your business name and location on all the major search engines. You should be found by your business name, but then search 'childcare in your location' and see whether you still come up. One way to make sure you start appearing is using keywords and tags on your website and any blog articles that you have. Be sure to use keywords like those listed below, along with your business name and location and any country-specific words used to describe childcare. Childcare, preschool, day care, toddler care, best daycare, best nursery, preschool program).

Online Directories

Take advantage of all the listings available to your business. Most of them tend to be free listings, but some do require a small payment. Of course they vary for each country, but here are some that I'm personally aware of - Yell.com, Craigslist, Daynurseries.co.uk, Angie's list, Citysearch, greatschools.org, Netmums, care.com, yelp.com, manta, foursquare, elocal, daycarematch, daycare.com. Most of these listings offer you the opportunity to get reviews from customers, so even though it's great being listed on all of them, you've then got to get the reviews on there too, otherwise if someone finds your listing without a review it could have a negative effect.

Develop Your Relationships

Introduction

So you've got a new child enrolled in your setting, but now maintaining great communication with the parent is going to be essential to not only ensure they stay happy and informed but to whether they recommend you to friends and family. There's no point spending money on marketing if we're going to be losing them once they've become a customer. In this section, we're going to take a look at ways you can develop your relationships with the parents and then encourage them to recommend you to others.

Parent Newsletter

Newsletters are a great way to communicate with parents, especially when you physically print them off and mail them home, instead of just emailing them. They are far more likely to read it if it comes through the post and is bright and colourful with lots of great content. We have children excited to receive it, especially if their work has been featured, or it was their parent's birthday. Everything that's happened for the month goes in to keep your parents up-to-date on all the great work you've been doing in your setting.

Here are some ideas you could include in your newsletter:

1. Room of the month competition
2. Birthday celebrations - children and parents
3. Any new updates within the setting (equipment, resources or technology)
4. Upcoming events
5. Thank yous for referrals in the month (including photos)
6. Art work of some of the children
7. Team member of the month
8. Activities you can do at home with your child
9. Any new blog articles you've created
10. Results of any competitions
11. A referral offer that parents can hand to a new prospect

Here's a great example of a monthly newsletter. It's bright and colourful and packed full of great content for parents to read. It doesn't need to be big and you can get 100 of these printed overnight for around £25. Remember to always include a call to action and get them out to businesses on your dream 100 list.

Cash Referrals

One of the most powerful strategies we've ever used is cash referrals. So, if someone refers a new starter, they get £30 for the number of days they are attending each week. So if a new child joins for three days per week off the back of a referral, the referring parent gets £90 cash. Would you be happy acquiring a new customer for only £90? That's nothing in comparison to how much money that parent is going to spend with you during their time as a customer. Take this to the next level by making sure you take a picture of you giving the money to the parent and then share it on Facebook and tag them in. You'll get more of your parents referring, and you'll also find the person receiving the cash will usually bring you in additional referrals very quickly over the next few weeks because you've motivated them to do so.

Collect Referral Stamps

You've probably seen those cards given by coffee shops - get a stamp every time you buy a coffee, then when you collect 10, you get a free coffee. Well, the same principle applies to parents making referrals.

Create your own referral card, when they make ten referrals they get 1 of 5 choices as an ultimate reward (everyone has different tastes, so they won't be all motivated by the same incentive). So still give them cash for each referral, but when they get to 10 referrals, reward them with something special.

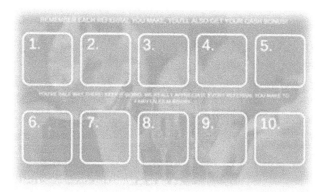

Give your team the best incentives

Typically childcare practitioners are not paid the best rates, so whatever referral incentives you have in place for your customers, take that to a higher level for your team. So you may offer £50 per day for each referral instead of £30. It's a great way to show your team that you really care about them and a great opportunity to earn additional cash and get them to really praise your setting to their friends and family.

Golden Tickets

Remember the Golden Tickets from the film Charlie and the Chocolate Factory. Everyone was after those golden tickets, so you could create your own version of this. Every time a new parent enrols in your setting you give them 2 Golden Tickets that they can share with any of their friends or family looking for childcare.

The Golden Ticket entitles the new parents to a huge offer, while the referring parent gets an equally great offer. It could be £300 cash. So, once the parent has liked your Facebook page, you can tag them into a post welcoming them to the nursery and mentioning the Golden Tickets to share with their family and friends. It always generates a huge amount of interest from their family and friends and always leads to an enrolment. Plus it's great publicity for your setting.

Of course, there needs to be terms and conditions around this, like they must enrol for a minimum number of days, but it's up to you to determine what they are.

Badges

I got this idea originally from a well-known theme park in Florida. They have people working there from all around the World, so not only do they have the person's name on the badge, they also have where they're from.

It has a huge impact, as people see the badges and strike up a conversation either because they're from the same place, they know someone there, or they're genuinely interested. We didn't think it would have the same impact on our setting when we first started using them, as all the team are from within a 15-mile radius, but we were surprised to see the number of conversations it triggered amongst parents and the team.

So, include your logo, name, location and perhaps something quirky about that person. I guarantee it will get people talking inside and outside of your setting.

Top Quality Parent Communication

New software solutions now give us the ability to communicate within seconds to update parents on how their child's day is going. Think about this scenario, parents are new to your setting and are nervous about leaving their child. Their child cries when they leave, and they're worried throughout the day about whether they've made the right decision. In the past, you would take photos and show them at the end of the day. Now we have the technology to send parents photos of their child having a great time throughout the day, helping put their mind at ease. This software also allows parents to easily add to their child's learning journey. You can use the system to update parents on new sessions available, events coming up, or send a group message specifically to that age group. It not only helps build relationships but is a great way to communicate with your parents.

Magical Birthdays

If it's a child's birthday within your setting it's your opportunity to make them feel really special. Birthday sign in reception, they get to sit on a special birthday chair, you buy them a present, they have a little tea party, you take lots of photos to send to the parents. Why not put in place a birthday protocol to ensure you're always prepared and each child gets the same experience. We've had parents call us up after their child's birthday in the setting to thank us as their child hasn't stopped talking about the amazing day they've had.

Greeting Cards

How many businesses that you buy a product or service from actually do anything for your birthday, or mother's day? Ok, they may send you an automated email, but that's about it. What if you sent out a handwritten card for each celebration. How special would that make your parents feel? They're more than likely to tell a lot of their friends and share it on social media. It's a small gesture but will really make your parents feel happy.

Create brand ambassadors

Most businesses having at least one or two raving fans that will do anything for you, as they love what you do. If you've got those raving fans, make them brand ambassadors for your business. Wine and dine them, incentives them and make sure they attend all of your events. We have a sash that our brand ambassadors where - Saying - I'm a mom at Fairytales - Got a question - Ask me. This works really well as many prospects sometimes feel they  can talk to them more than they can talk to members of your team as they feel they'll be more open. Your existing parents also come to them with ideas and suggestions, or if there's anything they're not happy with, so they're a great asset to have in your business.

In-house advertising

Parents are coming in and out of your setting every day, so make the most of this by positioning leaflets and promotions, or a television screen in prominent positions throughout your setting that they are bound to see when they are entering and leaving. You may want to promote a new stay and play session, or a new referral program. If you've got staff members make sure they are fully briefed on all promotions throughout your setting so they can answer any questions that parents may have.

Share Your Stories

The first piece of marketing I ever created for our setting was our origin story because people buy from people and not companies and they become more engaged and trusting when they can relate to you. I wanted parents to know exactly why we set up our business. I wanted them to know that my wife was so nervous about going back to work and leaving our children in the care of a stranger, and we couldn't find a childcare provider locally that had the same ethos as us. I wanted them to know our mission and our bigger purpose. I wanted them to feel more connected to us as the owners and feel they have that personal relationship. Now there are lots of stories that you can tell like - why you decided to open your own setting, why you fell in love with childcare, why you've picked the great team that work with you based on their stories. These stories help develop a relationship with the prospect, so take the time to write out your stories and share them with everyone.

Buyer's Remorse

As mentioned before, deciding on the right childcare provider for your child is the biggest emotional decision of your life. If you have parents who are really concerned about leaving their child, they may make the enrolment, but never decide to turn up, or pull out at the last minute. It's important to reassure them as much as possible. Sending them a welcome pack with extra goodies and a comforting message reassuring them can help. Include video testimonials from other parents who were apprehensive about leaving their child for the first time and how their child has progressed so much since they made the decision.

Here's an example of how one setting goes one step further and gives out a parent comfort pack on the first day their child starts, as they know parents will still be nervous and may still want to pull their child out of the setting if they feel guilty. There's a hand written note in there from their child's keyworker, a tea bag and a bar of chocolate, reassuring parents that their child will be loved and cared for and will have an amazing time.

Incentives Reviews

Reviews (social proof) from others is far more effective than us saying something good about our own business. One of the ways to get more reviews is to incentivise your parents. We produced a postcard that we hand out to five parents each week (putting reviews on gradually throughout the year is far better for Google and Facebook rather than asking everyone in the setting to do them all at once. It's a lot easier to chase parents up when you are only chasing a few each week). The postcard asks the parents to leave reviews on our top four websites (Facebook, Google, Day Nurseries and Yell.com). We give the parents clear instructions on how to complete the reviews on the reverse of the card. If the parent completes all four reviews, they get a £10 gift card as a thank you. If the parent makes a particular reference to a member of the team, the team member gets an extra £10.

It's easy for your customer to complete and they are incetivised to do it. If we receive ten reviews in a month, the team get an extra bonus. Making the process as simple as possible for the customer is key, so rather than make the customer search for our business on each of the platforms, we created a short bitly link directly to the specific page. That way, all they had to do was copy the short URL link and it would take them straight to the appropriate page.

Phone Enquiry

Introduction

The phone enquiry is often a part that lets a lot of businesses down and can often be someone's first contact with our business, so it's key to making a great first impression. In this section, we're going to take a look at how to deal with a phone enquiry, how to get all the information we need from the caller and give the caller the best possible experience during the call.

Answer the phone

Missing a phone call can mean missing out on a customer that could be worth over £30,000 to your business, so it's crucial to make sure your phone always gets answered. Of course your priority is the safety of the children first, so if you know there may be times when you  can't answer the phone, then you need to put backup processes in place.

Some settings divert their phones to a professional call handling service if they don't manage to answer in 5 rings. The answering service uses the same script as the setting and then pass the message on to the management team via a text and email. Another option is to have an auto attendant when someone rings - so instead of the traditional dial tone, you customer immediately gets greeted by a professional voice-over asking the caller to bear with you as someone is currently on the phone, then include some promotional messages about your setting while the caller is waiting. This is all going on while the phone is still ringing in your setting and waiting for someone to pick up. That way it buys you a bit more time if you are busy. Of course, you'll still need to have a professional voicemail for out of hours and those odd occasions that you just can't get to the phone.

Phone Script

The goal for all new telephone enquiries is to get the enquirer's contact details and to get them to book a trial. The problem is that when you're working in childcare, you're never just on the phone. Someone maybe at the door, children are crying around you, a parent's arrived to drop off a child and it doesn't end there. You and your team need to have a structure to follow, so no matter what's going on you know the information you've got to get. There are six core steps that will ensure you get what you need and the caller leaves with a great impression of your setting and professionalism.

1. Give them an AMAZING introduction - You want your prospect to hear the excitement in your voice that you're so pleased that they've called and you'd like to be the first to welcome them to your setting
2. Discovery - where you find out why they called you and where they got your information from
3. Rapport building - where you take the time to listen to the parent and show compassion
4. Communicate your unique mechanism - what's unique about your setting from the competition
5. Book the tour - it's important that you book the tour or get their contact information to send out your pack

6. The close - making sure you've answered any of their questions and they're happy and looking forward to the tour.

You can find out more about our sales training by visiting **www.childcarebusinessgrowth.com**

Train your team on how to handle a phone enquiry

It's so important to train your team on how to handle an enquiry over the phone, or in person. I've been in some settings where team members won't answer the phone when the manager is away as they are too scared to do so. It just comes down to providing the appropriate training to your team. Use part of your team meetings to always rehearse the script and role play. You could provide your staff with a certification for completing sales training (in telephone enquiries and face to face), which could be used towards their CPD.

Enquiry Tracking Sheets

This sheet is as important to me as giving feedback to a parent on their child's day. The whole idea of the tracking sheet is to ensure we capture all the relevant information from the prospect during the call and to find out exactly how they heard about us. Knowing this is crucial to determine which of our marketing efforts are working the best, so we can invest more into them. These enquiry tracking sheets should be located in every room, so they're easy to grab when an enquiry comes in.

Pricing over the phone

There are varying opinions on whether you should or shouldn't give out your pricing over the phone. Personally, I have no issue with giving an indication of pricing, as I don't want to waste time giving someone a tour who is purely judging us on price. Yes you might get the odd person who comes along who was originally looking for the cheapest provider, but then falls in love with your setting and enrols, but that's not going to happen often if you've done a great job marketing your setting before they call. They should already have an idea of what sets you apart from the competition. So, if someone calls and asks for pricing, we ask them if their decision is purely a price based decision or based on high quality and the unique benefits our setting can offer them. That way you're intriguing the prospect to want to find out more. Then we say that we can happily share our pricing during a tour. If they're still persistent and insist on pricing before they move forward, we say "Our pricing ranges between ___ & ___. Does that suit your budget? If so, we'll continue following the script and push for the tour. If they're not ready for the tour, we use our back up and offer to send them out a parent pack.

Incentives them to book the tour

Remember our goal from the phone enquiry is to get the prospect's contact details and get them to schedule a tour. Some enquries maybe a little hesitant at first, so it's important to have a few incentives that you can offer to encourage them to say yes. You could start by telling them you only have three slots left for tours this next week as you're getting a lot of new enquiries, or inform the prospect that you're availability is very limited in that age group; so you'd really encourage them to secure a tour before they're all taken (we always want something more if there's a chance we're going to miss out on it). Then you could offer them a free children's and adult's goodie bag if they have their tour before _____date (you could give them a date 7 days from now).

Prevent No Shows

We all lead busy lives, and things can crop up, so there's a chance that a prospect might forget to turn up for their tour, so you need to try and prevent this as much as possible. First schedule reminders for yourself to text the prospect the day before, then call them on the morning of their tour to remind them of their appointment and that you're looking forward to seeing them. When you're booking the tour for the prospect, you could politely remind them that your tours are in high demand and if they have to cancel or reschedule for any reason that you'd really appreciate it if they could let you know so you can offer the tour to another parent waiting. That way the customer knows your tours are in high demand and they feel more obligated to let you know if they can't make it.

On hold Audio

If you ever have to put a customer or prospect on hold at any time, make sure you've got a professional audio recording that they can listen to that plays calming music and talks about any offers or promotions you've got going on in your setting. You can get these call recordings produced very easily through 'on hold' audio companies. There's a great company I'd recomment using that has done all of our automated answering and the owner has created a special offer for all readers. Head on over to **ww.inarratoronhold.com/childcaremarketingideas**

The Tour

Introduction

This is the part that can either secure you the enrolment, or if it doesn't go well, the parent could end up telling others about their bad experience, so it's crucial to get this right. We're going to look at everything from conducting the tour, to how you should ask for the enrolment and then the follow-up. I'd encourage you to check yourself off against each one of these and give yourself a rating of 0 - 5. 0 = Not doing at all, right the way up to 5 = fully in place and happy. That way you can always come back and check your progress against each point. Let's get started.

Pre-tour call

It's always a good idea to call the prospect a few hours before the planned tour just to make sure they are still coming and confirm they know where they are going.

Please Their Senses

Think about the last time you walked into a new restaurant and how you created your first impressions of that business. First, you may have judged them on how it looked from the outside. Did it look clean and welcoming? Then as you walked in you would have been hit by the smell. Did the smell of delicious food excite you, or was there a smell of burnt food in the air. What did it sound like? Was it loud with great music, or was it so quiet you could hear a pin drop. Did you have to stand up to wait for a table or did you have a comfy sofa to enjoy some pre-dinner drinks? Finally the food, how did it taste, was it warm, did it fill you up. I'm sure you can relate to those sensations, and the same applies to when someone is viewing your setting. So use the following to see how you do against the five senses:

SIGHT - What do people see as they approach your setting and when they enter the building. Is it bright and colourful, clean and tidy and somewhere you'd like to send your child.

SMELL - As you open the door, what does it smell like. Is it fresh, musky, or is there a hint of dirty nappy in the air.

SOUND - Have you got calming or happy music playing, or are you drowned out by the sound of babies crying.

TASTE - Do you provide your prospects with a drink and perhaps some freshly cooked biscuits from the kitchen before the tour.

TOUCH - Have you got somewhere comfortable for the prospect to sit when they come in or are they stuck standing in the hall.

All these senses have a considerable impact on your prospects first impressions of you and your business, so it's important to regularly assess yourself against these and always be looking for ways you can improve on them.

First Impressions Count

So, we've covered off the five senses on the initial first impressions, but it doesn't stop there. Now it's time for the tour to begin, so here are some suggestions to assess yourself against -

1. Are the children happy ?
2. Are your team members happy and interacting with the children
3. Are they presentable and welcoming when you introduce them to the prospect ?
4. Are your display boards up-to-date and representing what you're currently doing in the setting ?
5. Have you got a display board purely for parent updates ?
6. Are you readdressing their concerns or questions that they raised in the initial assessmen ?
7. Is the outdoor space well maintained and all the equipment in a good condition ?
8. Do you have all your certificates on show ?
9. Have you pointed out the things that make your setting unique (and the benefits to the customer) ?
10. Is there lots of evidence that your setting is a fun, family-friendly place ?

Thank you cards work wonders

If you've got any thank you cards from happy parents make sure you have them clearly displayed for your new prospects to see when they arrive at your setting. It's more social proof that you provide a great service.

Personalised Greeting note in Reception

I picked this idea up from visiting my old account. Every time I would go there they would have a personalised message for me upon arrival. So if you know you've got a viewing today make a personalised welcome message for the child and parents - 'Welcome Zak and Maria to _____'. During the rest of the time, you could just have a generic welcome message to welcome everyone into the building. A great way of doing this is on a light box.

These light boxes are very cheap and the text can be changed very quickly to help that prospect feel even more amazed when they walk through the door.

Use their name

If you know you have a viewing booked, make sure your team knows the name of the child and the parent. Addressing someone by their name gives them comfort and makes you look more competent. According to research hearing our name lights up different parts of our brand that no other words do. It helps you like the person addressing you by your name and makes you feel more important. So make sure you and your team know the name of the prospect before they attend their tour.

Video Card in reception

When a prospect first arrives at your setting, a great way to ensure they know what you're all about it to sit them down with a drink and let them watch a video card. A video card is like an A4 brochure with a video inside. You can include a video from you introducing the setting and what you're all about, testimonials from parents and perhaps some short videos from key members of staff within the setting. The videos can easily be changed if you have a new message you want to get across. It's a great way to introduce your setting and leave the parent watching for a few moments while you do final preparations for your tour.

Find out exactly what they're looking for in a setting

Traditionally when a prospect attends a tour we are eager to share everything about why our setting is so wonderful, but we are missing the most important step. We need to find out exactly what the prospect is looking for. They may have had a terrible experience with another setting, or this may be the very first setting they've viewed. So, before starting your tour sit down with the parent and ask them open-ended questions about what they are looking for in a setting. You'll be surprised at how much they open up. Now that you know exactly what they're looking for and what their concerns are, you can make sure you address those points in the viewing. So, if they're concerned about safety, talk about how you have the best security system. If they are looking for their children to be pushed, talk about how the extra specialists that you bring in to enhance the children's learning. You can pretty much guarantee that the majority of other settings in your area are not conducting this initial assessment, so it immediately puts the parent's mind at ease that you are taking the time to find out exactly what they want. All this additional information will help when it comes to the close, so you can reconfirm to the parent that all the concerns they had have been addressed and you have everything they were looking for in a setting.

Get Everyone to Shake Hands

Of course, the safety of the children comes first, but if safety allows, I would make it compulsory that everyone you introduce to the prospect on the tour shakes the prospect's hand. It portrays confidence in you and your team and it's another thing that will help separate you from the competition.

Nuture Relationships

While you are giving a parent a tour of your setting it's important to give them time to talk with the key members of staff that will be responsible for their child, so they get the time to start to develop a relationship with them. Remember this is a huge trust based decision, so allowing extra time during the tour to spend with these key people is going to help build that trust. Allow them to trial the food and meet the cook and introduce them to other key members of your team like your parent partnership coordinator. Yes your tours may take a little longer, but you'll develop a much stronger relationship with the parent in comparison to any other settings that they have viewed.

Golden Tours

If a parent attends a tour and joins - mention if they get a new customer to join in the next 30 days, they get X% off their first month. You need to show some caution here and set some percentage limits and rules because you could end up giving a full-time parent 50% off their first month, but they only referred someone that signed up for one day a week.

Give a Goodie Bag

We all love receiving gifts, so at the end of the tour give the child and parent a goodie bag with an age-appropriate gift (educational or fun based), some branded merchandise and some inexpensive items like a colouring book and colours. For the parent, you could put in a small pampering gift from one of your local business partners. It's another way to set you apart from the competition and get those parents talking about you.

Here's an example of an overnight bag provided by a hotel that we stayed at recently. It had all the products produced in the hotel's brand, along with branded slippers to make the stay even more comfortable.

What could you do to surprise your children and parents with a branded goodie bag?

Mail a gift

If you don't manage to get a parent to enrol during their tour, you could mail out a gift the very next day. This could be something simple like a children's toy or a book, some chocolates for the parents and a letter to the parents saying it was great to meet them and reconfirming anything they raised during the tour. It helps show that you really would love to have them join your setting and you don't just see them as another enquiry.

Your Appearance

This might sound obvious, but do you have a strict policy on uniform and staff appearance. It all reflects on how the customer judges you on their first impression. If your team's uniform is looking old and dirty, parents may start to question what other things are slipping within your setting. What happens when your staff leave for the day. Do they continue to wear their uniform because their actions outside of work will reflect on you if they are still wearing it. Having a strict policy in place on the standards you expect can really help to make a great first impression on anyone that comes in contact with your brand.

Ask for the enrolment

This often scares a lot of people when it comes to asking for money, but you have to look at it from a different angle. If you think your setting is the right place for a child, where they'll get the best care and education, then you have a duty of care to ask for the enrolment. It's important to finish the tour by bringing them to a quiet room/area where you can ask for the enrolment. Tell the parent you think their child would blossom in the appropriate room and you'd love to get them enrolled today. You can put their mind at ease as your setting has everything they are looking for and then discuss the pricing. This will be uncomfortable at first but the more you practice this, the more you'll get used to it. Remember if you think you've got the best solution for that child, you have a duty of care to ask for the enrolment.

The Follow Up

You may show parents around your setting who just simply aren't ready to enrol yet. They may have only just had their baby and are looking at their options, so having a thorough follow up campaign is crucial to securing that enrolment. Ideally, this needs to be an automated system that schedules reminders and sends emails for you and arranges a series of follow up tasks. A sample campaign might be -

Day 1 - Send a toy or book for the child and some chocolates for the parents with a personalised letter telling them how much you loved meeting them.

Day 2 - Send an automated email sharing testimonials of why other parents chose your setting and invite them to give their feedback on the tour. You can do this by taking them to a simple online survey.

Day 3 - A follow-up call to make sure they got the gift and answer any additional questions that they may have.

Day 5 - Send an automated email sharing a list of what sets you apart from other settings and encouraging them to secure their enrolment.

Day 8 - Send a handwritten postcard telling them about any new and exciting developments you've got planned and you'd love them to enrol in the setting.

Day 13 - A follow-up call to see if they'd made a decision and to invite them in for a stay and play session.

Day 22 - Send an automated email with video testimonials on why parents chose your setting.

Day 35 - A follow-up call to see if they've made a decision.

Day 57 - Follow up email - Did we do something to upset you? (This email gets the highest responses. People apologise for not responding sooner and tell us they are still interested but have been very busy).

Day 60 - Move them to monthly email updates and include them in the newsletter mailing list (and still call them each month).

Ok this may look a little long and perhaps a little over the top, but we've had parents enrol almost six months after their initial tour, so it's important to keep in regular contact with them. Otherwise, there's always a chance they'll go elsewhere.

If you'd like to find out more about our automated campaign that you can use in your business, visit us at **www.childcarebusinessgrowth.com**

Social Media

Introduction

There are over three billion internet users, and over two billion of those have active social media accounts. So, the way we communicate with our audience has changed forever and avoiding social media as a business is no longer an option. The great news is social media provides your business with so many advantages over those businesses who are not embracing it to its full potential. In this section, we're going to take a look at why social media is so important and how you can use it to market your business.

Facebook Business Page

Setup a Facebook business page first, that way you can keep your personal and professional profiles separate. Here are some of the great reasons to have a business page.

1. You get increased exposure to potential customers.
2. You can gather more leads through your page linking to enquiry forms.
3. You don't pay anything to have it.
4. You can start to run Facebook ads and reach your specific target audience.
5. You can drive more traffic to your website.
6. You can share events you've got coming up and invite people to attend.
7. Keep an eye on your competition and how their page is growing.
8. Use Facebook insights to get a better understanding of your page.

Facebook Posts

It's important to keep your content relevant to your target audience. Remember your existing parents will be looking at your posts, along with new prospects. So, start with all the basics like:

1. Promote events and post photos from those events.
2. Host competitions and announce the winners.
3. Share tips and ideas on activities to do with your child, or child development.
4. Share photos of things you are proud of within your setting. That might be display boards, or new equipment you've bought.
5. Showing photos from charity fundraising also helps raise awareness for the charity you are supporting.
6. Post around four times per week and keep the content fresh. Opinions are different on this, but we've typically found around lunchtime and 7-8pm gets the best engagement from parents just after they've put their children down.

Facebook Insights

This is a powerful tool provided by Facebook, that gives you easy to understand data about users on your facebook fan page or group. You can track post engagements, which is a great way to see what your audience is reacting to. You can also look at the demographics of the users liking your page (gender, country, age range). Knowing this data allows you to tailor your message and then target your ads to appeal to more of the same audience.

Google Analytics

This allows you to look at data on the users of your website. You need to copy the Google code onto your website first, but then you'll be able to look at all the demographic data of users and the flow of how someone has gone through your website. You can see which pages are more popular and where people drop off, and you have the option to retarget them based on actions they did or did not take.

Optimise Your Bio

Adding keywords to your bio will help you show up more often in search results. Include phrases that your audience will be searching for – Childcare in 'your area,' Childcare options, Best Childcare in 'your area.'

Encourage Check-ins

You could design a simple backdrop that encourages people to take selfies or share photos on Instagram and Facebook. You could run competitions rewarding parents for the most shares, or the best selfie pic using your custom backdrop.

Run Competitions

There are plenty of people you could ask for freebies from - suppliers or local businesses, particularly those looking to promote their services to your audience. Plan out a competition at least once a month and relate it to a theme going on at that time. You could encourage your parents to create something with their child at home and share it on your group. Then you can respond and tag them in so all their friends and family can see.

Promote Your Audience Not You

We all love a bit of praise from others, particularly when our friends and family get to see it. So help them out! Congratulate parents and carers for taking part and attending events, entering competitions; anything where you can praise them and tag them in so friends and family get to see. If you have team members, praise and reward them as well. Your audience is far more likely to share these posts over self-promotion, and it shows you care about your customers and your team.

There's always room for self-promotion

I know this slightly contradicts my previous point, but I have a reason. If you've got good news stories, or you're offering a new add-on service, go ahead and promote it. After all, you're a business, but it ideally needs to be something newsworthy, such as a Good inspection report, or a new training course you've attended to better educate their child.

Tap in to communities / tribes

Where do your 'ideal customers' hang out?
Marketing isn't just about promotion "Me Me Me." It's important to interact and add value. Start hanging around where your ideal customers are - face to face locations or online in Facebook groups, Twitter chats just to name a few. Once you join those communities, start helping others and adding value wherever possible. The more you help others, the more people will start to know, like and trust you and promote you to others. You'll also start to see what problems or desires those customers have, which can then allow you to tailor your products and services accordingly.

Boost Your Facebook Posts

If you see people are liking and engaging with your posts on Facebook, start to boost them as a paid advert. It's a really easy process to follow and you choose who you want that boost to be shown to. So, people similar to your existing customers, people with children, people who have liked your page, people within a certain area and age range.

Ask People To Share

There are lots of ways we can encourage people to share things, but one of the most successful ways is by playing on people's emotions. So, if you've got good news stories, or perhaps you're looking to raise money for a local charity, or praise for one of your parents, then people are more likely to share this over a post that is trying to sell a service.

Engage in Conversations

If you've tagged a parent on a post to congratulate or praise them for something, you'll often find that friends and family will like and comment on that post. You can then message that person and encourage them to like your Facebook page.

Ask for Referrals

This is one of those things that we often forget to do, or avoid doing for fear of making the customer feel awkward. A simple way to do this is add a Call To Action (CTO) at the bottom of the post asking them to share it with others who they think might be interested.

Run a Poll

One of the best ways to get feedback and engagement from your group is to run a quick poll. You may want to get an idea for your next blog. Ask them what topics they would like covered and give them some suggestions. It's important to respond promptly though and praise people for joining in and contributing.

Set up a Social Pod

If your Facebook or Instagram posts aren't getting much interaction, then you could create or join a pod. Pods are simply groups of people who like and share each other's social media content. You want to work with others who have the same target audience as you but are in a completely different industry. An example of this might be an indoor play centre without a nursery or creche.

Post content frequently and encourage engagement

Some people think that they don't have enough to share with others, or they don't feel they've got anything to share at all. One of the things we need to realise as a childcare professional is that we've got a lot of knowledge in our heads that most parents don't know. Think back to your training and share your thoughts and opinions around this, or activities you can do at home.

Schedule posts

The last thing you want to be doing is manually sending all of your social media posts out, especially when there are some great online systems that will do this all for you, like Hootsuite and Sprout Social. These platforms are easy to set up, you just copy and paste your content, along with the photo, and you tell it when to send the post. Right now, the best time to post is usually lunchtime and in the evenings when the children are in bed, so make the most of scheduling your posts, so you also get a bit of downtime.

Use Facebook Live or Instagram Stories

Facebook loves video, so if you can share content live with your audience, there's more chance of people seeing it over a static post. You can also boost it later if the video gets a good response. Another option could be to record a live tour of your facility after the children have gone home. Share stories adding value and sharing your knowledge with your audience.

Survey Parents

The great thing with online surveys is parents are more likely to respond when they've got time and they're scrolling through Facebook, rather than asking them for feedback as they're rushing out the door. We regularly get lots of comments from the parents around how they love being involved in the decision process, so it's a great communication and feedback tool.

Facebook Team Page

If you've got members of staff set up a team Facebook group for them. It's a great way to bring the team together to share ideas and praise them at random times to show them how much you value them. You can run team competitions on there, such as the best resource found for outdoor play, or the best new blog post. If we're looking to add a new piece of equipment or trial something new, we'll often run polls on there asking their opinion. That way they know they've got a say in the decision-making process and they generally tend to be more open on the page instead of asking them face to face. It's easy to set up and can really help motivate your team.

Facebook Pixel

The Facebook pixel is a piece of HTML code (website coding) that you copy and paste onto your website. It allows you and Facebook to track what people are doing on your website and the type of people visiting your website. That way, if you ever decide to run Facebook ads to your website, Facebook will already have a good understanding of the type of people that are likely to take action on your website, and they'll show your ads to more people in that target audience.

A good way to check if you've got the pixel code installed on your website is by downloading the Facebook Pixel Helper. This is a little icon that sits on your internet browser and shows you if the code is installed on your pages.

Facebook Bot Messenger

Facebook Messenger bot gives you a private message channel directly to your user. The message appears straight away in their Messenger app, so it's a great way to get past all the clutter of email and social media. You'll need an existing Facebook page to set up its bot functionality and you'll need administrator rights on the page. You can answer customer enquiries in seconds and send out offers, promotions and events to your existing list. There are lots of companies offering this tool and one we are using at the time of writing this book is **www.manychat.com**

Linkedin

Even though Linkedin is mainly for business to business use, it's important not to dismiss it as a great marketing tool. You never know who might decide to take a look at your profile, so it's important to keep it up to date with all your professional qualifications and any testimonials you can get from other business professionals that you have worked with. You'll then want to set up a business page that shares all your core content - company introduction, what you're about and any contact details. Share your blog articles on your page. It all helps position you as the local childcare expert. If you decide to target corporate companies in the future, you've now got a good presence online that they can review and may be more likely to take you seriously when you approach them.

Youtube Channel

At the time of writing this book almost five billion videos are watched on Youtube every single day and over 300 hours of video are uploaded to YouTube every minute. So if you're not on Youtube you're missing out on a big opportunity. Youtube is owned by Google, so having videos on Youtube that are set up with the relevant keywords will help your listing. Set up your own Youtube channel and get uploading. There's lots of great content you could share on there:

1. Parent testimonials
2. Tours of your setting
3. Advice and guidance on childcare related topics
4. Graduations
5. Event photos
6. Updates about your setting
7. FAQs from parents

Direct Mail

Introduction

Over the last few years, the amount of direct mail we receive from companies has been decreasing, but in recent times it seems to have flipped full circle. Businesses have realised that since the general public is receiving less, they're more likely to open it when it does arrive and looks enticing. Did you know that Google advertises their Google Pay Per Click service via direct mail to businesses? So, if the online giant of advertising is using direct mail, there's clearly something in it. In this section, we're going to take a look at the various ways you can communicate with your enquiries and existing parents via direct mail, so let's get stuck in.

Lumpy mail

Most of us like getting mail, as long as it's not a bill, but we're even more intrigued when it's something bulky. We just have to open it out of curiosity. There are lots of great little products you can put in the mail, like a blanket, mini sand timer, small toy, dice, bottle, or pacifier. The key is to tie your marketing message back to the product.

For example - You could send them a sand time with a core message around time is running out to secure your place, or a stress ball with the message around there's no need to stress anymore now you've found the right childcare provider. You're pretty much guaranteed someone is going to open it, so you need to make sure you've got that strong message inside and remember to follow up a day after it arrives

Here's an example of a lumpy mail I just received whilst I was writing this book. As you can see, you just have the urge to open it.

Mailing out products

I talk about this in the lead magnets section in more detail, but if you've run an advert giving away sample products, like a baby security lock, that person has given you their address details and is expecting the product to be shipped to them. So, when you mail the product out to them, you could include a quick introduction to your setting and make sure your message relates to the product.

For example: Hi Mrs. Smith, thank you so much for requesting this baby security lock. Here at _____ we take the security of children in our care extremely seriously and have a ten point security protocol to ensure all children are kept safe at all times. If you'd like to find out more about _____ we're currently running a great promotion this month where we include a home security pack (worth £99) for every enrolment in the setting. We'd love you to come and take a look around _____ at a time convenient for you. Give us a call on _____ to arrange a viewing.

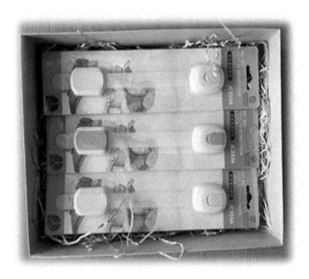

Flyers to popular areas

If you've identified through your map areas where a high number of existing parents come from, be sure to mail them regularly with different promotions letting them know others in the area are already using your services. Be sure to always include a call to action - 'Go to _____ to download your holiday voucher worth £50. Hurry though as there's only 20 available'.

Send out a parent pack

One way to really stand out from the competition is to create a parent pack. This is a bright, colourful cardboard pack that is posted without being put in an envelope. Traditionally companies in most sectors send out a brochure in an envelope, so you can guarantee that when this arrives through the door, it's really going to stand out from the competition. This is our most popular request from our website, and we'll usually tend to deliver it on the very same day if the request has come in before we've gone home for the day (I talk about this elsewhere in the book). The great advantage of sending a physical pack instead of emailing it is that you now have their address to send them further bulky mail if they haven't requested a viewing from the pack. However, we've been sending the pack out for the last four years, and we've consistently got 94% of those requesting a pack then booking a viewing, so I know it works really well and none of our competition is doing it to this level.

It has lots of great content in there including -

1. An introductory letter telling our story with a family photo.
2. An eight-page brochure all about our setting and the curriculum we provide.
3. An A3 sheet full of testimonials front and back.
4. A checklist on what to look for in a high-quality setting.
5. A USB stick with an introductory video to our setting from us the owners along with parent testimonials.
6. Our pricing presentation along with mission and values.
7. Tea bags and a bar of chocolate for the parent to enjoy while they read through the pack.

Post-tour gift

Whether you enrolled the person or not following the tour I would always say to send them a gift the very next day. For the child, I'd recommend sending a small toy or book, and I'd send some flowers or chocolates for the parents. I'd include a personalised letter either welcoming them to the setting (if they enrolled), or thanking them for taking the time out to view your setting (if they didn't enrol). Again, not many other companies would consider doing this in any industry, so it really helps you stand out from the crowd.

Postcard follow-ups

Postcards have been fading out for some time as most of us tend to use social media to keep everyone up-to-date on our adventures. That's why I still love to use postcards, particularly oversized postcards with bright, eye-catching images, so they immediately grab your attention when they come through the door. Another great thing with postcards is that you don't have to open anything to read what's written on the back. So a nice quick message following up on an enquiry, or a quick thank you note for helping out at an event is just another great way to get your brand out there and keep in regular contact with prospects and existing customers.

Here are some examples of postcards that Tricia Wellings and her team from Bright Kids nursery send out:
1. A thank you for visiting card – please come for a free trial – to all visitors who have not booked.
2. A thank you for registering – now recommend a friend and receive a gift.
3. A thank you once they have recommended one – to encourage them to recommend another one!

Greeting Cards

How many businesses that you buy a product or service from actually do anything for your birthday, or mother's day? Ok, they may send you an automated email, but that's about it. What if you sent out a handwritten card for each celebration. How special would that make your parents feel? They're more than likely to tell a lot of their friends and share it on social media. It's a small gesture but will really make your parents feel happy.

Printed Material

Introduction

The benefit of having printed materials and merchandise is that it gives you an opportunity to constantly be promoting your business to anyone who comes into contact with one of your branded merchandise pieces. So, if you've got children walking around with your branded hoodie, or parents driving with your sticker in their window it's constantly promoting your brand for free. Yes, you've got the initial cost, but that piece of merchandise may still be seen by new prospects two or three years from now. So in this section we're going to take a look at some branded materials you could be using.

Business Cards

You never know when you're going to meet someone that might need your services, so it's important to always be prepared and carry professional, eye catching business cards with you at all times. Of course you should include the basics, but why not take it further and make it into a foldable card and include a few good comments from your

Ofsted report and a link to a free report that they can download. That way you're encouraging them to take action. You can also treat your business card as an appointment card, so write a time down that this new person you've just met could come in to take a look around your facility. They'll be a lot more likely to turn up if they think you've scheduled an appoitnment specifically to see them.

Water bottles

These are great for parents and children. Parents will be able to use them for work and the gym, whilst the children will be able to use them whilst out on field trips. They're constantly being seen by new prospects and it's another great method for helping spread your brand and how you feel on keeping hydrated.

Stationery

Let's face it, most of us love receiving new stationery and resources, so it's great if you can apply your logo and then give out your branded stationary to your existing parents, prospects on viewings, new starters and local businesses on your dream 100 list. That way you're giving them all something for free, but in return they are spreading knowledge of your business to their network.

Some of the things you could include are:
1. Mouse mat
2. Pencils and pens
3. USB sticks
4. Drinks flasks for parents
5. Children's bags

Here is a great example of a company sending some mints, a tea bag, lip balm, a note pad and a pen, all in one smart presentation pack that explains what each of them are for.

Bags

Giving a branded bag out when a new child starts your setting is a great little thank you gift that parents will love to have. You then get several children being seen with your branded bags on the way to and from your setting.

Clothing

Some childcare settings choose to have a uniform which is a perfect opportunity to present your brand, but there are lots of additional opportunities to present your branding on clothing. You could have a funky hoodie made for your children or a group t-shirt if you and your families decide to do a local event together.

Postcards

We talked about postcards earlier, but another way to use a postcard is if you're running an event that you want your existing parents to promote; this might be a summer fayre. Have the postcards pre-written and stamped, then give them to your existing customers to send out to their friends and family to invite them to the event on your behalf. The new enquiry then brings that postcard with them, and the existing parent gets a special thank you gift in return.

Advertising Colouring Pages & Crayons

Creating your own drawing pad that you can leave in waiting areas (of doctors, or dentists) for children with branded crayons is a simple way to promote your brand. Take this one step further and have a call to action by getting parents to take a picture of their child's drawing to enter a competition. The parent likes your Facebook page and then uploads it to your Facebook page to enter the competition.

You then announce the winner each month and tag the parent in so all of their friends and family see it.

Promotional pens

If you're anything like me, you're always looking for a pen. They're a great giveaway to all your parents and prospects, but also to local businesses. It subconsciously gets your name out infront of a lot more people.

USBs

Even though USB sticks have become a very common freebie, they still carry some value to the prospect, as they can use the USB for additional storage. Plus it's a great opportunity for you to put some video content on there and send it out with the parent enquiry pack. You could include a brief introductory video from you and why you setup your business, testimonials from existing customers and ideally a main video showing lots of happy smiling children and staff within your setting and the great resources you have available.

Designing your own marketing material can be very expensive, so we've saved you the trouble and developed a series of templates that are already done for you. You just load the template and insert your own details. If you'd like to find out more, head on over to **www.childcarebusinessgrowth.com**

Paid Advertising

Introduction

In the past everyone needed big advertising budgets to get their message out to their audience, but that's all changed. Digital opportunities are available to every business, they're easier to track and can deliver a great return on Investment (ROI) and they allow you to increase or decrease the amount you spend at the click of a button. So, if your setting is full you could decide to decrease your ad spend, or increase it if your numbers are low. Here are some ideas on how to use paid advertising in your business.

Facebook Ads

Facebook ads are adverts you create to target your ideal customer online and are displayed in either the news feed on desktop, news feed on mobile and the right hand Facebook column on desktop. Here are some of the reasons why Facebook advertising can be such a great investment.

- **Audience targeting** - You can create custom audiences based on things people have declared they like - for example 'Pareting, childcare, toddlers'. Facebook also has a huge amount of aditional demographic information that other platforms simply don't have. For example they know gender, geographic location, age, relationship status, education and profession. This is just to name a few, but I've included a list below of some of the information you can use to target your audience on Facebook.

- **Easy to setup** - The structure to set up ads and campaigns is not much different than posting a post, so you don't need advance knowledge or code to get it started.
- **Low cost** - Even though the cost is rising as more businesses turn to Facebook ads, the cost is still relatively cheap to reach your target audience with this level of accuracy.
- **Retargeting** - You have the ability to retarget people based on what actions they have taken and choose what content to show them.
- **Socially engaging** - If someone else has already liked the ad, it provides social proof to others.
- **Variety of ad options** - You can use still images, or videos to test which work better for your target audience.

Here are some of the targeting options Facebook has to offer:

- Location

- Age - the ability to select an age range

DEMOGRAPHICS -
- Gender - male, female or all
- Languages - any language
- Relationship - 'Interested in' or 'Relationship Status'
- Education - level, field of study and schools and undergrad years
- Work - employers, job title, industries,
- Home - home type, home ownership, household composition
- Generation - Baby boomers, Generation X, Millennials
- Parents - Parents of children of particular ages, types of moms
- Life events - like new job, new relationship, upcoming birthday, away from family

INTERESTS -

- Business & Industry - banking, construction, small businesses
- Entertainment - Games, live events, movies
- Family & Relationships - fatherhood, motherhood, marriage, parenting
- Fitness & Wellness - dieting, gyms, nutrition
- Food & drink - beverages, cooking, cuisine, restaurants
- Hobbies & Activities - arts and music, home and garden, pets, travel, vehicles
- Shopping & Fashion - beauty, clothing, shopping, toys
- Sports & Outdoors - Outdoor recreation or sports
- Technology - computers, or consumer electronics

BEHAVIOURS -

- Business To Business - Industry or company size
- Charitable donations - type of charity
- Expats - multiple countries
- Financial - banking, investments
- Mobile Device User - by brand and type of device
- Purchase behaviour - types of things they buy
- Travel - business or personal, family vacations, frequent flyers
- This isn't everything, but it gives you an idea of how detailed you can get with your targeting.

Facebook Retargeting

Once you've got the Facebook pixel installed on your website you can start to run Facebook retargeting ads to those that landed on certain pages of your website, but didn't land on others. Think about it, how many times have you been looking at something on the internet, got distracted and then forgotten all about it. This allows you to show reminder ads to those that didn't get to the page you wanted. So, someone might start to download a free report from your website, but didn't get to the thank you page. You could show them that report through an ad and link them back to that specific page. It's a very powerful tool when it's used correctly.

If you'd like to find out more about Facebook advertising and retargeting check out our online training courses at: **www.childcarebusinessgrowth.com**

Google PPC

This is my favourit advertising platform. Why? Even though the cost might be slightly higher than other platforms, It allows you to target people who are actually interested in your services and are actively looking right now. So if someone is on Google and types in 'The best childcare in Birmingham' they are more than likely trying to find childcare in that area. They are actually looking for information right now. That's why Google PPC is great because you are targeting someone who is actively looking for what you provide. Why not go to Google and type in - 'Childcare in your town' and see what comes up. You may find some of your competitors are already advertising on there, so make a note of what they are saying in their adverts. You may find no one is using PPC, so it's a great opportunity for you to take the number one spot.

Make a list of words and phrases you think a parent would type in if they were looking for childcare in your area. Type those words and phrases into Google and see what other ideas come up. If you can't find an advert - make your search a little bigger, so you include a local city. There's bound to be someone using PPC then. Have a look at what they've got written in their ads, so it gives you an idea of what to include in your advert. Remember to be specific on location when you're setting up your ads. The last thing you want to do is show your ads to someone living 100 miles away from you. I wouldn't spend too much right out of the gate. Start with £5-£10 per day if it's your first time using Google PPC. Keep a close eye on how they are performing. Google is great at giving you feedback.

It will show you which keywords you appeared for and people clicked on and a whole heap of other information. You can also adjust your bidding and daily spend. Google PPC is definitely one of the best forms of advertising by far.

If you'd like to find out more about running Google PPC ads, head on over to **www.childcarebusinessgrowth.com** to find out more.

Youtube Advertising

YouTube has a total of 1.3 billion users and is the world's second most used search engine at the time of writing this book. It's the third most visited website after Google and Facebook. Youtube adverts are generally still cheap, in some cases ads will cost you as little as a few pence. If you use TrueView ads you only pay when a user watches 30 seconds or your entire ad, so you never pay for impressions that don't keep viewers watching.

Targeting on Youtube is very good, you can target your audience by age, gender, keywords and parental status. However, that's just the beginning. You can show your ads on specific videos, channels or websites. So if you know your prospects are looking at videos specifically relating to parenting or childbirth, you can get your video ad in front of them.

Partnership and Networking

Introduction

One of the biggest realisations I ever had in marketing was that someone else has already got my ideal customers. So relating this to parents, they may already attend play centres, play groups, doctors, dentists, sporting clubs. The list goes on. Partnering with others allows you to build your network and access their customers via a referral directly from that business they are already buying from. Let's take a look at a few examples.

Dream 100

Your ideal customer is already someone else's customer. So, they're already buying products or services from someone else. They could be a mother to be going to pre-natal classes with a personal trainer, or they could be buying baby clothes from your local  clothes store. I call these businesses part of my Dream 100 List. They are all businesses that already have my ideal customer and I want to create a relationship with that business, so if their customer is ever looking for childcare, they'll recommend me. Here's some examples of who might be on your dream 100 list - gyms, salons, toy stores, blog writers, doctors, play centres, dentists, mother and toddler groups, children's hair salons, estate agents. Any business that already has your ideal customer and doesn't offer the same product or service as you. Building a relationship with these dream 100 list is key to get them referring into your business.

Attend local network events

Chamber of Commerce and BNI are great examples of networking events. These are all great opportunities for you to make other local businesses aware of your setting and why you stand out from the competition. You'll be surprised how many of the other businesses attending already have your ideal customers and could refer you quite a lot of business. Who knows, you may find a business service there that you need.

I've been to these events and people in the room, or family members were looking for childcare at that particular moment in time. Ok, that's not going to happen every time, but it's worthwhile giving it a go. Be sure to try out several groups before committing to anyone in particular. The great thing with these events is that they only tend to have one business from each sector attending to ensure that you get the best return from your investment. Personally, I would suggest trialling several local groups before you commit to anyone in particular.

Here's an example from Nicola Taylor at Ashbourne Day Nuseries at Little Acorns. Nicola and her team attended a local children's centre open day. They had a section where they set up some activities with colouring in and pencils for the children. They also set up a display table with a pop up banner and large poster highlighting their services. They received four enquiries on the day and one enquiry through their Facebook advert about the day. They got one enrolment and the rest were all for babies looking for next year, so potentially more to come. They took the enquiries details down and have kept in touch with follow up calls inviting them in for a visit. Great job for a few hours work.

Get interviewed or interview them

There are a number of ways to do this. First of all you need to contact the radio stations and position yourself as the local childcare expert and if they ever need someone to interview in childcare related topics then you are happy to help. The same applies to television with more local television stations popping up, so it's easier than ever to get on television. You have to have the brass balls to contact these channels and offer your services as the local childcare expert, but the publicity from it can have a major impact on your business. The second way to do this is if you've got a strong opinion on something that's topical right now, then make your opinions known. Don't be afraid to sit on the fence. Share your opinion and let others know how you feel. It may get picked up by the media.

Contribute to publications

Editors are always under pressure to produce content. They'll happily publish quality articles for free. What publications and blogs do your ideal customers read, then reach out to get in front of them. Don't worry if you're not good at writing content. You don't have to write it yourself. You could hire someone to do this for you as a ghost writer. You tell them exactly what you want and they write it for you. You then have content ready to share to other publications.

Affiliate Programs

This is another form of joint venture; similar to the Dream 100 List, but all these partnerships will be after is a commission in return. So, these types of partners exist in two core areas - Those with a big following in your sector, simply looking to promote a product in return for a payment. The second type of affiliate are those that are affiliates for a living. They will actively go out and promote your brand on your behalf through various forms of advertising, again in return for a commission payment. The important thing to remember here though is you give them strict parameters on what they can and cannot say. The benefit is that you have a sales team at your disposal, but only pay them for sales.

Build relationships with other professionals

Do you ask on your enrolment forms for medical information, including doctors and dentists names and locations. You can tell parents that you need the information in case of an emergency. You may find that a lot of your families use the same dentist, so it would be great to form a partnership with them. Approach the dentist and let them know that a number of children from their practice come to your setting and you'd like to work with them to ensure you're doing everything possible to promote healthy teeth. This way it shows the dentist that you're setting is very popular with their patients and that you care about the health of the children's teeth. Why not invite them or one of their colleagues in to deliver a talk to all your parents and children. That way, they also get to meet other potential parents at your setting. You could start this relationship by delivering a parcel of fresh fruit and a note explaining the message above. Make sure you follow this up if you haven't heard from them.

Contact Large Local Businesses

Getting your services listed on the employee benefits program is a great way of potentially accessing a lot of parents. They may already have a solution in place, but acting as their overflow is still a great opportunity. The employer will be looking at why they should partner with you, so having an exclusive offer is going to be key to sell the program to the decision makers. Another important factor is making sure that your package is right for them. Think about hospitals for example, or factory workers. They have lots of parents working there will unsociable hours, so can you offer a flexible package for them. Schools are another scenario, because they may only want childcare during the school term. Once you've got a partnership in place, you really want to try to arrange a presentation to anyone interested perhaps during their lunch hour, or they may invite you along to employer fairs. Make sure you take plenty of professional marketing and have your offer ready to present. This probably isn't going to be something that happens overnight, but you never know, you may call an employer at the right time when they're looking for a solution.

Partner with Local Estate Agents

If people are moving to the area they may not yet be aware of the childcare options around them. So partnering with local estate agents gives you the opportunity to impress them even before they've moved in. You could offer a special rate exclusively for moving day. It helps make the estate agent look great for arranging it for them and it gives you an opportunity to impress the parent's right from the start. You could also offer an exclusive package for the first month. Approach the estate agents by taking in a nice gift, it could be some freshly baked cookies from you to sweeten them up and make sure you approach them in person and not just via a phone call.

Partner with Local Restaurants

A lot of restaurants offer free meals for children on their quieter nights, so you could approach them and offer to provide them with a member of your team to run kids activities at the restaurant on those quieter nights. If you've got team members this is a great opportunity for them to earn some extra cash.

Photographer

You may already be bringing in a photographer to take pictures of your children, but what about them promoting you in return. You could offer them a cash incentive for each referral, or the opportunity to be on your membership card to encourage parents to use them. Whatever you do, make sure it's trackable so you can thank the right person.

Wedding venues

If there are any wedding venues nearby you can approach them and offer your services as a wedding creche. This is not only a great opportunity for you to promote your business to parents attending the event, but it can provide a great additional revenue stream for you. We got started by offering our services for free for one wedding to a local wedding venue.

They were so pleased with the results that they now recommend us to all the weddings held at the venue.

Write for the local media

This is a great way to be positioned as a local expert. Local media - newspapers, articles, websites and blogs are always looking for content. Don't be afraid to be confident in your opinion. There's no money in being neutral, so if you have an opinion on something, be proud to share your thoughts, knowledge and opinion. You'll get lovers and maybe some haters, but you'll start to position yourself as the local childcare expert very quickly.

Partner Referrals

One of my favourite films is Miracle of 34th Street and I'll always remember the part in the film where Coles would help their customers find a product elsewhere if they didn't stock it themselves. I'm not suggesting you tell parents to go to another setting, but you may not cater for a particular age group, or you may be full for that age. If you're working in partnership with another nursery and recommending them potential customers, then they may feel obliged to do the same in return. If someone does something nice for you, you feel obliged to give back. Of course, you need to build this relationship, but I have seen this happening in a few childcare settings and both partners benefit from the relationship.

Community Marketing

Introduction

There are so many opportunities to develop relationships with your local community, and the great thing is, it's going to cost you hardly anything except time, but will bring you a great return on your investment. How great would it feel if someone new to your community asked about where to find the best childcare and everyone highly recommended you? That's the benefit of community marketing, so let's take a look at how you can develop these relationships.

Free Friends Day

Invite your customers to bring a friend on a traditionally quieter day of the week where you can host a stay and play session. Make sure you collect their contact information to follow up and present them with an offer.

Hand out fruit as well as flyers

Rather than just handing out flyers to prospects at events, why not give them a piece of fruit. It helps you stand out from the crowd, and you can tie in your marketing message about how all your meals are healthy and nutritious.

Advertise in Apartment Blocks

Large residential blocks are a great place to get your message out quickly. Most of them tend to have central mailing areas in the lobby, so you could personalise a flyer to mention the particular apartment block, "Lots of other Chesterfield residents love attending our nursery. We'd love to invite you along for a stay and play session on _____ Call us on _____ to reserve your space." It's a quick way of getting your message out to a lot of potential customers and presenting them with an opportunity to trial your setting with other people from the same apartment block.

Monthly Cake Runs

Wouldn't it be nice if you were a local business that received a treat once a month from your local childcare expert. A great way to do this is to schedule a cake run. Select 5-10 businesses on your dream 100 list and take them out a box of treats once a month. You could buy them from a local baker (one of your VIP partners), or get the children to make them. It's important to do this consistently, so the business starts to look forward to them. It's guaranteed to start a conversation, and if anyone ever asks them if they'd recommend a childcare setting, you know who's going to come front of mind.

Here's my wife with a box of Krispy Kreme for one of our dream 100 partners who we know love receiving them every month. So far that business has referred us eight childen, all for the early cost of £120 on Krispy Kreme once a month.

Contact Local Groups

There are usually lots of groups that already have your ideal customers attending them, so stay and play groups and parent clubs. You could contact them and ask to pop along to introduce your setting. If you're more confident, you could offer to do a talk on a particular topic that's relevant to them. Sourcing these groups is one job that could be passed on to a virtual assistant.

If you'd like to get our guide on hiring a virtual assistant visit **www.childcarebusinessgrowth.com**

Partnering with new building sites

New residential building sites usually mean new people are moving to the area. So offering the sales team an exclusive offer for people moving into their homes is a great way to get in front of people who may not have heard of you yet. You could offer a special moving day rate to help the parents out during that stressful process.

Partner with your local library

Ok libraries aren't as popular as they used to be, but a large number of parents and children still use them, and they often tend to invite schools and childcare settings in for activities. So let the library know how much you appreciate them by regularly taking them some tasty treats and giving them some flowers. If other childcare practitioners are using them, then you need to stand out from the crowd and go those ten steps further to make them feel that extra bit special. So, the next time anyone asks them which childcare setting they'd recommend, it will be you coming to the front of mind.

Don't forget to include lots of promotional materials to leave them on the counter.

Partner with local schools

If parents have children attending school, then there's a good chance they may also have a younger child. Putting on talks or workshops for parents at the school is a great way to reach a large number of people that may need your services, or know several other people looking for childcare. Teachers are another great example. Why not create a term time offer exclusively for teachers. We do this every year with our local schools and the head teachers always support us by putting up flyers and posters and personally handing out letters to teachers who may be looking to return to work following the birth of their child. Another way to further show your support for the local schools is to help out at local fayres. Again, make the most of the opportunity with your own brand clothing, lots of promotional material and a competition to gather everyone's details.

Partner with local Colleges and Universities

There are some great ways to build relationships with them. First of all their staff may need childcare, so put in place an exclusive discount purely for that College or University. Try and get a slot where you can get to stand in front of them and tell them about your amazing setting. You may find students are looking for childcare. The ideal opportunity would be to sit down with the Principal or Dean to arrange an exclusive discount and the student funding support. It's far better to do this face to face with the decision makers and then arrange to present your setting, either via a live face to face presentation, or a pre-recorded webinar that they can watch at their convenience. You may struggle to get the College or University to exclusively work with you promoting your programs, but you could offer the Principal / or Dean a partnership; for every student that brings their child to your setting, you offer one of their students a work placement in exchange. The leadership board will be happy with this if they see that their learners are secruing a work placement opportunity with each referred enrolment.

Align with a charity

Having a greater purpose and a story behind your business plays a key role in attracting new customers, building loyalty and ultimately helping change the World. You can arrange fundraising events, get the local press involved and really help make a difference to a local cause.

Here's great example provided by Kelly Finsky Corke-Withany from Busy Bees. They set up a giant relay between five nurseries. They advertised that they would be doing it on Facebook, along with lots of local selling and events pages. They borrowed a shopping trolley from a local supermarket and filled it with goodies and information about the charity they were raising funds for. The staff dressed up in bright colours and strange outfits to promote their USPs, so the uniforms reflected these. They put up posters, advertised the event on their website, made a justgiving page and shared it everywhere. On the day the girls walked armed with lots of goodies, which they gave out to adults and children, along with information about childhood meningitis and the signs, (their chosen charity was a meningitis one) and they were armed with a loudspeaker to attract attention!

They've had more than double the amount of enquiries each month since the event, along with parents mentioning seeing the girls out during their initial visits to their setting. The event also received press attention so they had great coverage. There was a minimal cost implication to this event, as they had to buy some of the goodies that they gave away, the outfits were home made and the other resources were either borrowed, or at the nursery anyway, so a very small cost. A great example of taking action and doing something different to stand out from the competition."

Interchangeable text sign

We are constantly bombarded by advertising messages everywhere we go, so we end up becoming oblivious to the adverts around us (we become ad blind). So if you're in a location where the same people pass your signage every day, they're not going to pay attention to it if it stays the same day in day out. So, using an interchangeable text sign allows you to mix your message up. You could come up with all sorts of lines to keep your message original and quirky. Your sign will stand out from the competition. Here's a couple of examples:

1. What will your child grow up to be when they're older?
2. Love changing nappies? We do…
3. _____ where every day ends happily ever after
4. We're sorry you're going to work while we're having fun
5. Your child is in caring hands
6. _____ preparing your child for their next adventure
7. Have fun at work…..We will…

Press Releases

This is a great way to share good news stories with your community and get some free publicity at the same time. The local media are always looking for good news stories that they can share, so take advantage of this great opportunity. Here are some examples you could be sharing with the local press.

1. Holiday fayres
2. Events where you've raised money for charity
3. You could host a best fancy dress competition and encourage people to vote online
4. Anything you've contributed to the local community
5. Parent celebration events
6. Award nominations or certifications

Start by searching online for the contact details for each newspaper. Put them in an Excel file; so every time you've got a new press release you can send it straight to that list, then set a goal on your marketing calendar to submit one new press release every two months. Remember to invite the press along to take photos of any extraordinary events that you're doing.

What Makes You Unique?

Introduction

It isn't enough these days to just offer high-quality childcare; customers expect that as the norm. They want to know what separates you from the competition and what unique benefits do you provide for them and their child over the competition. So, in this chapter, we're going to be looking at ways to make you unique and set you apart.

Add an Air Purifier

New technology is emerging all the time and at the time of writitng this book, air purification units are the new thing. I'm not just talking about those ones you can get for your home. I'm talking about large floor or wall mountable units that you can get that contain a UV filter. So, this is another opportunity to impress parents that you have gone further to prevent the spread of germs within your setting.

Add a Steriliser

One of the biggest concerns parents have with childcare is the risk of their children catching viruses, so you could address this by putting in an electronic sterliser. I'm not talking about a bottle sterlisers, I'm talking about a unit where you can put in toys, bedding, pretty much anything and dry sterlise it. At the time of writing this book these are very rare in childcare settings, as they are very new and appear expensive, but we sourced ours directly from the manufacturer in China.

Workshops for Parents

Offering workshops or courses for parents to attend for free is another unique benefit that most other settings still aren't doing at the time of writing this book. I talk about this more in another section, but the key here is to ask your existing parents what they would like to attend and then look into whether putting on that event is feasible. We trained a member of our team to be paediatric first aid qualified so we didn't have to pay an outside provider. Now parents can complete the basic course for free, or pay just to get the certification on top.

Happiness Guarantee

Finding somone to look after your child is the most important decision you will ever make, so anything you can do to eleviate the parents concerns that their child is going to receive the best quality care is going to be a huge plus. Money back guarantees are proving very popular in most industries, but they're still very rare in childcare. Why not apply the same guarantee to childcare, but give it a friendlier name - Our Happiness Guarantee - If you're not 100% happy with the care your child receives within the first 30days we'll give you a full refund. This might scare some of you, but if you're confident in the service you provide and you don't have people ask to leave you in the first 30 days, then why wouldn't you offer this guarantee. It will shock parents that you're offering such a guarantee and the reality is parents don't want to move their child once they've found the right childcare provider.

So, the majority of starters will never use this, but I can pretty much guarantee that it will encourage more parents to join your setting, because of the confidence you are portraying in your service. You want to put this guarantee on every piece of marketing and make sure it's always discussed confidently with the prospect.

Membership Discounts

The majotiy of us like to receive discounts, so why not create a membership card for all parents that use your setting. As parents to children, we all have a list of companies that most of us will usually use during our child's upbringing. For example - party supplies, bouncy castles, hair salons, shoe shops, birthday cakes, to name just a few. The idea is these companies will form part of your Dream 100 list and you approach them to give you some sort of discount for you promoting their services to your customers. You could promote them on a TV screen in reception and through your partner brochure. You then give your customers a VIP membership card and a list of all the discounted companies that you work with. Your joint venture partners will get more business, they'll promote you to potential parents and your parents will get some great savings in return and feel valued.

Membership area online for parents

If you're not already using a childcare software package where you communicate with parents online, you could create a parents membership area using a software like Click Funnels. You could include all bonuses in here exclusive to your parents. It might be a free onine first aid course, baby development, food hygiene, anything you can get of value.

You could also included all of your newsletters, vouchers and offers to share with other parents, updates about the setting and pictures of your setting's events. It's a great USP to offer over your competition.

We've already built a membership template for you. All you need to do is add your own details and content.

We've also added some suggested topics. You can get ahold of your template by visitng: **www.childcarebusinessgrowth.com**

Promote recent investments

If you've spent money on new equipment, resources or training, then let everyone know about it. Explain what the benefits are for them and their children. Help your customers see that they're getting more value for their money. It might be obvious to us, but sometimes we need to spell it out to help people truly appreciate the investment. You could do this via photos or video and post it on all of your social media channels. You may have new animals at the setting, which you could let parents and their children name via a Facebook competition. You may have new resources for the children. Anything you think parents will be interested knowing that will benefit their child.

Here's a five minute video my wife and our parent partnership coordinator filmed to let parents know about our new garden area and ask them for feedback on what they'd like to see.

Your Unique Mechanism

Most childcare settings are high quality these days, so being high quality isn't enough to set you apart from the competition. Of course parents are looking for the core things like safety and a friendly atmosphere, but they also want to know what's unique about your setting and the way you deliver your program. This is one reason why it's so important to know what your competition are doing, so you can better understand and rely what's unique about your setting. So some examples of what's unique about your program could be -

1. You have a woodland area with an outdoor classroom
2. You might use a combination of two childcare practices
3. You may have specialist providers come in to your setting on a weekly basic to enhance the children's learning.
4. You maybe the longest running setting in your area
5. You may have more years experience than any other provider
6. You may provide additional classes - like baby massage or yoga
7. You maybe a family run setting
8. You may have a high tech security system

If you don't have a unique mechanism then you may need to invest some time and money into finding one that separates you from the competition

Features versus Benefits

One of the key things we need to get right is the difference between features and benefits. A feature is a factual statement about the product or service being advertised (like a large outdoor play area). The benefit answers the customers' question, "What's in it for me?" So you have a large outdoor play area - that allows the children lots of room to run around, get lots of fresh air, explore, climb and grow their own vegetables. So I would encourage you to think about the things you point out on your tours. Do you just explain the feature, or describe the benefit. Here are some more examples of features and benefits:

1. Free fresh fruit at reception - so children and parents can grab them on the way out and help maintain a healthy diet
2. Free nappies and milk - saving you the hassle of having to bring them in each week
3. Free hot drinks for the parents - so you get time to grab a drink for yourself after you've dropped your child off on the way to work
4. Online software - so we can send you updates on your child throughout the day including photos and observations of your child's progress

Write your own book

You are already a professional in your area, but writing your own book helps positions you as an expert in your field and separates you from the competition. It's a great unique feature that you can promote at every opportunity, through press articles, speaking at local events and interviews. You could focus on a particular aspect of child development, or write about how to choose the most appropriate childcare for your needs. It needs to be something that people are interested in and want to find a solution for. You don't necessarily have to write the whole book yourself. You can hire a ghostwriter through somewhere like **www.freelancer.com** to do it for you. Once you've got your book you can give it away to all prospects on your tours, or use it as a lead magnet on your website, where you do a free plus shipping offer.

Know, like and trust

Introduction

Choosing the right childcare for your child is the biggest trust based decision you can make, so it's crucial that a parent develops a relationship with you before they trust you to look after their child. So, in this section we take a look at the various ways that you can start to get parents to know, like and trust you.

Video Testimonials

Video testimonials are my favourite type of testimonial by far. There's nothing better than watching a parent tell a story of how their child has grown and progressed since starting at your setting. Prospects watching these videos not only see a great example of social proof, but they can often relate to the points parents raise in the video. A great example is where parents describe how nervous they were about leaving their child for the first time and how they had nothing to worry about. Watching this parent tell their story and show their emotions helps a prospect relate to this and feel reassured that it will be the same for them.

You can use them on your website, Youtube channel, videos out to parents, social media platforms and you can upload them as a video to create a social media ad. A couple of tips for you - If you're holding any type of event where parents are coming along, this is the best time to get a number of reviews filmed in one go. I remember an event where my wife and I were at a graduation recently and my wife lined up nine parents in the space of 20 minutes to give us nine new video testimonials. Graduations are a great opportunity as parents are pleased with how their child has progressed and achieved, so grab them while they're in the right frame of mind. Another tip is to line up some questions that you'd ideally like them to answer. This way you can make sure you cover off all the fears or concerns a new parent might have.

Written Testimonials Wherever you can

The more testimonials you can get the better. Now my personal preference is raw videos, but of course, you can't put videos on printed material, and not everyone wants to watch videos. So written testimonials are great on any form of written marketing material. Here are just a few examples of where you can use them - on your website, flyers, brochures, vehicles, social media platforms, email signatures. It's important to include the person's name and location and a photo. This just provides more credibility that you haven't just written them yourself.

Keep your social proof up-to-date

We've mentioned earlier what others say about you (social proof) is far stronger than what you say about yourself, but this can also act against you if they aren't kept up-to-date. So, if you have great reviews on your website, but they are all two years old, that's going to leave your customer wondering what's happened to your business over the last two years. So aim to get at least one new testimonial a week. Just imagine, if you got one a week, you'd have 52 new testimonials by the end of the year. Plus Google and other search engines prefer it when you've got a steady flow of reviews rather than upload a pile of them at once.

Professional Video

I remember the first day we put our new video out to the public back in 2014. The impact it had on our business was just amazing. Prior to launching the video we spent a whole day planning it and arranging for parents to be onsite for the filming. The video cost us £4,500 to get produced by a professional videographer. Now you may think that was a lot (and you can actually get your video filmed a lot cheaper these days), but within the first three months of launching the video we secured over £52,000 worth of new business from the video (based on the average yearly value of a customer). That £4,500 investment has gone on to help generate over £540,000 in new sales (where customers have directly attributed the video to one of the main reasons why they enrolled). So, clearly video is key, as it immediately helps prospects take a look around your setting and see why other parents recommend you. Now video is one of the very first things I produce with my Inner Circle clients as we can get it produced quickly and start using it on our websites and in Facebook video ads.

If you'd like to find out more about our coaching and mentorship programs, head on over to **www.childcarebusinessgrowth.com**

Professional Photographs

I know a lot of people don't like having their photo taken, but if you were a parent looking for someone to look after your precious child, you'd want to know what they look like. So rather than search your phone for a good photo, I strongly recommend getting some professional photos taken of you and any team members. They don't cost a lot if you shop around.

While you're at it, don't just go for the standard headshot, get some fun shots of you laughing and joking around.

You'll never know when you'll want to use them in any of your marketing.

Blogging

FT002: NEW PARENTS, IT'S PERFECTLY OK TO LEARN ON THE JOB.

Becoming a parent can be daunting and exciting, but the desire to raise our children to the best of our abilities often leads them of us to rush to Amazon and start our life long student journey of parenting.

There's so much information available. Blogs, podcasts, vlogs and books go ..

These days we're all bombarded with emails and sales calls, so it's no wonder why people are more reluctant than ever to give out their contact information. We need to work a lot harder to get that information, and the best way to do that is by providing lots and lots of value. A great way to do this is through blog articles specifically related to your target audience.

Not only does it help you build a relationship with the prospect, but it can also help boost your search engine rankings if done correctly.

It's important to start by thinking of what information do parents want. This might be a problem they want solving, such as helping their child to sleep, or they might be looking for activities to do with their children. The great thing is you don't have to write them all yourself. You could hire someone to write them for you, or get your team members to help out by recording the activities they do in your setting and then transferring them into a blog article.

Remember, your target audience; a parent purely receiving funding from a deprived neighbourhood isn't necessarily going to be interested in the same topics as a parent from a wealthy background.

If you'd like a jump start, you can get your hands on some pre-written blog articles we've created to get you started. Head on over to **www.childcarebusinessgrowth.com**

Lead Magnets

Introduction

People are less willing now more than ever to give out their contact information, because they are constantly being bombarded with phone calls and emails and informaion overload. So the old days of simply having a form saying request a call back are long gone. Yes it may work on the odd occassion when someone is ready to buy, but what if you've just found out your pregnant and are just looking at your options. You're not even ready for phone calls or viewings yet, but you would just like more information. So, this is where things like lead magnets come in. Lead magnets are reports, PDFs, checklists; documents that people can get access to information that they want to solve a problem, in exchange for their email address.

Let me give you an example - If you're a new parent and you don't know what is the best childcare option for your child yet, you could provide a downloadable report that gives the pros and cons of each type of childcare. You're helping the prospect solve a problem, but you're asking for their email in return. That way you can start to communicate with them and develop a relationship with them over time by putting them on an automated email campaign. Now most industries have been using lead magnets for sometime, but 90% of the childcare sector probably aren't using any type of lead magnet on their website or other forms of marketing. So that's a big opportunity for you to take advantage of. So in this section we're going to be taking a look at the different types of lead magnets and how you can use them to attract more customers into your business.

Video Courses

These have become very popular, but are rarely used in Childcare marketing. It's a great way for people to get to know you in a short amount of time. You could do a short series of videos on a number of topics - Your story and introduction, why your type of childcare is important to a child's development, information of funded options, tours around each room, meeting members of your team. These would be free, but you could create short paid courses covering child development topics, or first aid, or activities to do at home. They're easy to record on your phone and can be delivered in a number of ways as a short course through Vimeo, or an online portal. You could even use them as part of a Facebook ad campaign.

Email Courses

This is similar to the video course, but the idea is that you automate the course through your CRM provider. You can breakdown the topic into small daily email lessons, so people can absorb the content in bite-size chunks.

Ebooks

Ebooks are a great way of adding more value to your audience by helping them solve a specific problem. This might be potty training, bedtime routines, or how to deal with tantrums. The idea is that it helps to solve that specific part of the issue. So you wouldn't look to cover all of those topics. Focus specifically on one and break it down into simple to follow steps with text and images.

Guides

This topic is quite vast, because there are so many potential topics you could cover, but the idea is you provide a simple step by step guide on that particular topic, so be as specific as possible. A good example would be a guide to potty training, which you could then use as a free give away to parents who are looking to potty train their child. Be specific on the topic and age range so you can use it as a lead magnet for that particular audience.

Free plus shipping

What items are cheap to get produced, but are in high demand by parents - things like door locks, or baby toys. You can buy them cheaply and give them as giveaways through your website and social media promotionals. The best way to do this is through is through a free plus shipping offer funnel. So you appear to give the customer the product for free, but you make the money back on the shipping. It's the same principle as giving away a PDF report or checklist, but you're making a sale to acquire a new lead and getting their address at the same time, so you can add in some promotional information about your setting.

Craft Booklet / Recipe Cards

As parents we're always looking for new ideas to do with our children. You could take photos of the activities you do within your setting, write up a description and put these into a booklet / guide for prospects to download from your website. You could produce a booklet that covers all ages, or be more specific and create a booklet for each age.

Challenges

Create packs that provide parents with challenges they could do at home with their children. This could be how to progress to writing their name in 10 easy steps. These can just be in a PDF format that can be downloaded from your website.

Local events & activity guides

We're always looking for new exciting adventures to do with our children, so how about creating a simple guide of places you can visit locally and events that are taking place over the next few months. You could go one step further and get a team member to contact the venues and try and arrange some sort of discount or offer for your parents. Share this with existing parents and prospects through your website and social media channels and encourage people to get in contact to get the file.

Checklists

Our most popular download has always been - What to look for in an outstanding childcare provider. Why - because when you first become a parent, you are overwhelmed by all this information that you need to know and what to look for in a quality childcare provider is one of those areas. This checklist shows that we are trying to help them by giving them advice and guidance, which helps them build trust in us as a provider.

Send to current lists

It's important to offer your lead magnets to your existing lists. You may have had someone enquire six months ago that was just browsing their options at the time and is now ready to make their decision. You may have a former parent who knows someone who could really benefit from that guide you produced. Staying in contact and providing them with value is key and it's free because it's all done through email.

Email Marketing

Introduction

Email may not be as popular as it used to be, but it's still an essential component of any marketing strategy. Your email lists are so important because it is valuable data that you own and control. Unlike social media where increasing costs, account bans and algorithms change, this is data you can communicate with for free and send a specific message to depending on the list they are in (former parents, current parents, old enquiries). Yes open rates have dropped considerably, so you need to grab attention quickly and stand out from the crowd. Here's a few ideas you could try

Automated Campaigns

One of the biggest missed opportunities I see in childcare settings is not having an automated campaign once someone has made an enquiry. So if someone downloads a free checklist or guide from your website, you've now got their email and can start to communicate with them with the goal of gradually encouraging them to book a viewing of your setting. You can share testimonials, USPs, all sorts of information over a period of time, starting with a subtle hint to book a viewing and then making that message clearer as time goes on. Personally our automations start asking them to book a viewing in the 2nd email.

Follow up automation campaigns

The automation doesn't need to stop there. So, if you didn't manage to get that prospect to sign up during the tour, you can then kick off another campaign, with the goal of getting them to sign up for your setting. Again, make sure you are sharing more valuable content on why they should choose your setting and asking them to fill out a survey of what they thought of your facility.

Use Welcome Emails

Even though you'll be calling parents and welcoming them to your setting, providing them with an automated welcome email can be extremely helpful to the parent. You can include all sorts of essential information, like what to bring on your first day, reminders for them to like your Facebook page and add you to their safe email sender list.

Include Emoticons in your subject lines

At the time of writing this book 95% of businesses are still using bland subject lines. Including an emoticon in your subject line will ensure your email stands out from the crowd. That additional colour will immediately grab attention and help improve the chances of your email being opened.

Eye catching subject lines

If you use the same old boring subjet lines as everyone else, your email is just going to get lost in the crowd. You need an eye-catching headline to help it stand out from the rest. Things like -bad news, I'm sorry, did we do something wrong. The email that gets the highest open rate on our first automation (driving someone to book a tour) is the very last email.

Change your email signature

 You'dbesurprisedhowmanybusinessesdon'thaveabasic email signature let alone adding these extra elements. Be sure to include your logo, social media links and any current campaigns that you've got running. Keep mixing it up every few months. Your email signature is a perfect opportunity to get a new marketing message across. We also have fairy characters for each member the team, since our setting is called Fairytales.

Create a regular newsletter

A printed newsletter is always better than an email newsletter because it's something physical that you hold and can mail to customers, but if you don't have the capacity for that, you should at least be sending an email newsletter. It's a great way of regularly keeping parents and prospects up to date with what's going on in your setting. Be sure to include valuable content, such as useful articles, a staff interview, child based activity; anything that your parents can get great value from. Yes, some self-promotion is ok, but keep this to a minimum.

Include P.S. Notes

Have you noticed how you always tend to read the P.S. note at the bottom of emails and letters? It's because it always stands out being away from the main text, so make the most of it. It's a great place to repeat the core message, or call to action of the email.

Gather new customers challenges

It's important to ask every new customer what their biggest challenge was when looking for childcare. Not everyone will reply, but overtime you'll get a clearer picture of exactly what challenges they had and why they chose your setting. You'll be surprised at some of the answers, but knowing this additional information will allow you to amend your marketing accordingly.

Use email as a voting system

This is another way to engage your customers in a two way conversation. Asking them questions on plans you have for your setting, new lessons you want to introduce, or ideas they may have. Engaging your customers shows you care about their opinion. You can use a link for each answer to make it easy to measure the result, or you could simply ask them to reply to the email.

Automation

You have to remember that someone may enquire about your setting in the early stages of pregnancy and is only now starting to look at their options. Unless you start to build a relationship where they can know, like and trust you over a period of time, it's unlikely that you're going to get them into your setting for a viewing. You need to keep communicating with them regularly with specific calls to action. The first is to try and get them into your setting for a tour. Once they've been in for a tour you want to drive them to enrol. Without some type of automation in place, it's extremely difficult to manage this. I've worked with some settings where they've had enquiries sign up 15 months after their initial enquiry, all because they kept communicating with them regularly and didn't give up. We've tweaked our automation over the years, but the email that gets the most response from parents is the one that is sent 54 days after the initial enquiry. We've created a series of automation templates that you can implement straight into your business. You can get a copy of them by visiting: **www.childcarebusinessgrowth.com**

Event Ideas

Introduction

The traditional 'open day' style events have gone, so it's time to be more creative. Events are one of my favourite marketing methods; yes they can be hard work, but they give you an opportunity to be creative, raise money for charity, meet lots of new enquiries, get great publicity and have fun with existing customers.

Date night baby sitting nights at your setting

Once a month you could offer your parents a premium service where you open for longer hours so they can go on a date night. This again is another unique benefit you can offer over your competition and could be something you open out to other parents in the area to encourage them to use your setting. You can guarantee they'll be telling others about this great new service.

Attending charity events with parents

Popping along to a local charity event with one of your parents to show your support is a great way for building relationships and showing you care about the local community. You could offer to support the charity as your nominated charity for the month.

Community Seminars / workshops

A great way to bring your target audience together is by putting on seminars and workshops for them to attend. Ideally you want to do it in your setting if you have the space, so they get to see your wonderful facilities, but holding them at a local venue still allows you to develop that relationship with the prospect. We host accredited courses on paediatric first. Why not run a poll on Facebook to your existing audience to find out what events or courses they would be interested in and then invite your prospects and existing customers to bring a friend.

Event creche

There are always local events going on that your target audience will be attending. Why not offer to host a creche at the event. It's a great opportunity to speak to lots of potential prospects and show how you interact with their children. Make sure you have lots of promotional material with you and enquiry forms that you can get them to fill in there and then. Take your goodie bags along and run a competition where everyone has to give their address to enter. That way you can mail them out something in the post later to follow up. You can also invite them to like your Facebook page, as you will be announcing the winner on Facebook.

Customer appreciation events

Put on a big fancy party for all of your existing parents and children to thank them for being part of your setting. Invite any partners you have along to give them a chance to meet your parents. So, if one of your partners is a bouncy castle supplier, ask them to come along and provide the bouncy castle for the children. Also invite any new prospects along so they can see exactly how you look after your customers. Host awards and get your local partners to sponsor them. You could even raise money for your local charity. Make it a big annual thing that everyone looks forward to.

Social events for customers

There are lots of opportunities throughout the year to invite your parents along. Parent socials, or family gatherings in the park, family trips. Halloween or Christmas parties. Encourage them to dress in fancy dress and then run competitions. Again it's a perfect opportunity to invite any new prospects and their children along.

Local children's retailers events

If you've got any local children's stores close to your setting - offer to provide a free creche on the weekend. You can sell it on the basis that you'll take care of the children, whilst it leaves the parents to shop in peace. Again, make sure you take lots of promotional material, grab their addresses and get them to like your Facebook page.

Local Community Events

School fayres, charity events, church events - they all have an opportunity for you to showcase your services and show that you support the local community. Be sure to take along some of your exciting equipment, work children have completed and lots of promotional material. Try and get one of your brand ambassadors to come along with you too. Be sure to host a competition inviting everyone to take part and like your Facebook page where you'll be announcing the winner.

Public speaking events

You may not be too keen on the idea of public speaking, but it can have a massive impact on your business if you can gain the confidence to stand up in front of others and talk about your business and share your expert knowledge of childcare. There are lots of groups for this, but one of the most universal around the world is a group called toast masters that help you develop those public speaking skills with others who are also looking to gain confidence in public speaking. I'd really encourage you to find a local group near you and give it a try.

Give your events a theme

Traditional open day style events are fading out, so why not give your event a theme. You could host a summer fayre, or a Christmas party where you raise money for your local charity. Invite your local businesses along and ask them to share some competition prizes. Tell your existing parents if they bring a friend, they'll both get a gift. Invite anyone that can tell others about your amazing facility. Make it a big event and invest some money into promoting it, flyers, Facebook ads, videos, put it as an event on your Facebook page and highlight all the great things that will be happening on the day. Bouncy castles, party food, competitions, prizes, animal man, disco. You want your event to stand out from the crowd and be the event everyone looks forward to attending each year. If you've got a cook - get them to come along and cook up some tasty healthy treats. Be sure to have your promotional packs ready and gather their details. It's a great way of getting prospects in without the pressure of being sold to.

Pricing & Packaging

Introduction

I've spoken to lots of settings over the last few years who are worried that their competitors are charging less than them and I say the same thing to all of them. It doesn't matter that you're charging more than the competition, as long as you can justify the price with a higher quality, unique service. The key thing to point out is there is no point trying to be the cheapest because as soon as someone else comes along and lowers their price, you're forced to do the same, and your profit margin suffers. You want to be in a position where your business is full, and you can continue to raise your prices due to all the unique benefits you offer your customers. In this section, we look at ways to present your pricing and create offers rather than discounts.

Time Sensitive Offers

Everyone likes to think they are getting a great deal, but that doesn't mean that you need to discount your prices. Constructing an offer, is thinking - what additional value can I provide to improve the perceived value of my package and encourage the customer to take action now. For example, you may include a promotional offer - sign up in the next week and get a goodie bag packed full of educational resources worth £97 and access to our online training platform worth £297, but you only charge them £89 on top of their childcare fees. The goodie bag and online training platform may have only cost you £10, but the perceived value to the customer was far greater, so the customer thinks they are getting a great deal and you get to pocket the extra margin.

Bundle Your Offer

We all like to feel we've had a good deal. I'm not talking about providing a discount here, as this just devalues your service. What I'm talking about is bundling things together to create an offer. So, including nappies, or food, or branded clothing as part of a package that is cheaper than buying them separately has been proven to increase sales (and of course increases your average customer spend). It's important to make it clear that the customer is saving money by buying these things together, so the perceived value is a lot higher. It also reduces the number of options the customer has to choose from, making the buying decision simpler.

Don't be the cheapest

I remember Dan Kennedy (a famous marketer) once saying, there's no strategic value in being the second cheapest in your market, and if you're the cheapest your competition may just keep trying to undercut you. Now you don't want to be the cheapest particularly in childcare, so be confident in your pricing and position yourself towards the higher end and justify to your prospects that not only do you provide the highest quality care, but you've also got several unique benefits over the competition.

Reframe pricing

Breakdown the cost into daily or weekly equivalents to help the customer get over their initial impression that something is expensive. Try to put it into context and compare it to something they can relate to. For example, if you are charging parents for meals - That's less than an a cup of coffee in Starbucks. Putting it in the contest of other comparable daily expenditure can make it seem much more affordable.

Free has no value

I often see signs saying FREE CHILDCARE PLACES and nothing else. If something is free, it instantly can appear to have no value. Start by replacing the word free with funded. Remember, it also needs to have a call to action - go here, or call this number to find out more, or to secure your place. This also relates to promotional offers as well. You could have the most amazing freebie in the World, like a free goodie bag full of great resources, but it will be perceived as having no value if it's free. Always give something a value. If it's an offer it helps when it's something tangible that they need to bring in with them like a printed voucher. Putting an expiry date on it also enhances the perceived value and gives people a deadline to take action.

Present three pricing options

When you offer three pricing options, it has been proven that the majority will go for at least the middle option. If you are only offering one price, the customer only has once choice. This also comes back to the 80:20 rule. 20% of your customers will be prepared to pay a higher price for a better product. Of course the care you offer won't be different, but a great way to do this is by having offers where you include additional items as mentioned above.

Price Guide

Having a professionally laid out pricing guide that is easy to understand is essential. The last thing you want is for your prospect to be confused. Show your pricing guide to others before you publish it to make sure they understand and don't have any questions. Remember to show additional pricing options if you're confident you can show the value.

Visual Cues

I'm sure you've seen pricing tables with visual cues like - Best Value, Best Seller, Most Recommended. These cues (visual or verbal) help guide the customer to your preferred products and prevent them from having to think too much.

Have a consistent discount rule

First of all, it's important to determine whether or not you want to give discounts. You may decide against them all together. It won't take long for a parent to share a discount with their friends if they think they've got a good deal. On the other hand, if one parent feels they didn't get the same discount as another, it could cause more problems for you. If you are going to give a discount, for example on a 2nd child, make sure it is always consistent and you always ask for something in return, such as a video testimonial.

Highlight your added value

Usually your customer will try and compare your price against your competition. This is why it is so important to point out the added value you are providing. This may be additional tuition like Spanish or music and movement lessons, or meals included. It's important to show this added value and this is another reason why it's so important to know your competition, their prices and the services they provide. It's so important to point out what separates you from them.

End your pricing in the number 7

Ending your price with 9 has subconsciously made buyers feel they are getting a good deal, even though £39 isn't much of a saving on £40. Personally I think using the figure 7 is now proving more popular and appears to show some additional thought in your pricing strategy.

Personal Development

Introduction

This book is packed full of helpful tips to market your childcare business, but none of them are useful unless you have the right mindset to implement them. Here's a couple of ways to help stay on track to grow a successful business.

Define Success

How do you know if any of your marketing activity has been successful if you haven't defined success? It might be the number of enquiries you get, or how many people turn up for a tour. You can't achieve a goal unless you already have a goal in place. Remember, this doesn't just apply to marketing. How else do you define success in other areas of your business and then share that with any team members.

Keep Learning

The same basic principles of marketing that applied 50 years ago, still apply to this day, but the way we continue to use those basic principles is constantly evolving. A great example of this - Pattern interrupt has always been an effective marketing principle (making your ad stand out from the competition). A great example of this was when video first came out as an option on Facebook ads. People were used to seeing images and then all of a sudden video ads started appearing and causing a pattern interrupt. These days, video marketing is common in most sectors, so people are now trying new ways to cause this same pattern interrupt. It's important to keep applying the basic principles, but staying up to date with the latest breakthrough techniques in applying those principles is crucial.

Targets in place

If you've got nothing to aim for, you'll probably not achieve a great deal. You and your team need to know what the target is for the month and year to ensure everyone is staying on target and incentivised to do so.

Implement to Completion

This book is packed full of ways to market your childcare business, but without implementation they are useless. So, I'd encourage you to tackle them one at a time and make sure you've fully implemented the task before moving on to the next one.

Attend events

I know we all lead very busy lives, but I cannot encourage you enough to take time away from your business and attend events. I used to be guilty of always making excuses that I was too busy to go, but I'd always be so grateful when I did go. Not only would I learn something new, but it would give me time to reflect on my businesses and not be stuck in the day to day running of it. I go back with a clear head of things I need to change or improve and it always gives me the inspiration to get back to taking my businesses to the next level. Why not check out what events we've got coming up over the next few months by visiting **www.childcarebusinessgrowth.com**

Surround yourself with like minded people

They say you become the average of the five people you most associate with. So, if you're not interacting with other childcare professsionals, or successful business people that you aspire to be like; then you're not going to develop. It's so important to interact with others you aspire to be like so they continue to inspire you to reach your own goals.

Accountability is key

One of the benefits to being your own boss is that you don't have to report to anyone, but that can also be a huge downside to running your own business. If you haven't got anyone to hold you accoutable, it's too easy to let goals and deadlines slip. I would encourage everyone at all levels of business to have some sort of accountability partner or mentor outside of your family and friends. Someone you know will help set you goals and hold you accountable to achieve them and work with you if you have a challenge with your business.

If you'd like to find out about our coaching and mentorship programs, head over to **www.childcarebusinessgrowth.com**

Tools & Resources

Fiverr.com

A great place to get tasks and services completed by freelancers from only $5.
www.fiverr.com

Freelancer

If you need a project completing, check out this site where you can hire a freelancer to do it for you.
www.freelancer.com

Provely

Allows you to put social proof on your website proving others are subscribing or buying your services
www.provely.io

Rev

A great transcription and translator service, so if you have videos or audio you need written down, this is the place to get it done.
www.rev.com

Vimeo

A video hosting and sharing website great for sharing videos with your team.
www.vimeo.com

Zotabox

A selection of tools to put on your website to help boost subscribers and sales.
www.zotabox.com

If you'd like to get more tools and resources for your business, then visit www.childcaremarketingideas.com/resources   to find out more

Cartoonist

Here's the contact details for my cartoonist if you'd like any cartoons similar to the drawings in this book.
https://www.fiverr.com/gadtoons

Voiceovers

If you'd like professional voice recordings for your business this is the guy I'd recommend.
https://www.inarratoronhold.com/childcaremarketingideas

Conclusion

Thank you for taking the time to read this book. Right now you're probably excited at the great opportunities to start marketing your business, but I'm sure you may also be a little overwhelmed with all the information. That's actually a good thing, as your brain has already started working out how you can implement these strategies into your business.

You should feel proud of yourself for sticking with this book right to the end. There's a lot of information that can make a big difference to your business, but only if you implement it. So, my advice to you is start right back at the beginning, where we discussed the Fundamentals. It's so important to get these in place so you've got a solid foundation before you start spending any money on marketing.

This book isn't something you just read once and go on with your business as usual. It's an implementation guide that you should keep handy and keep ticking each strategy off as you implement it in your business.

Once the first strategy is fully in place, then move onto the next one and just keep going. The good news is that most of the strategies in the Fundamentals section don't take that long to put in place, so you should be able to get through them quickly. Then, it's up to you which strategies you choose from there, as it depends on what you've already got in place. Perhaps you know you'd like to improve your social media, so start there, or you may feel that your competition is doing a great job with their direct mail, so start there. Each section in the book will deliver you results, so just get implementing.

I'd love for us to continue to build on our relationship together, so I'd like to present you with two amazing opportunities. If you'd like step by step instructions on how to get all of these strategies, and more, implemented in your business; then I've got a great offer for you. Our Childcare Business Growth System goes through each step in detail. I've even included a pile of FREE gifts (worth £1,497). Visit our website to find out more **www.childcarebusinessgrowth.com**

Now, if you want to grow your business faster and you just want everything done for you, I've created something special for business owners who just want it all taken care of. You'll get to work with me one on one and my team will take care of all your marketing.

If you're interested in being part of my 12-Month Master Plan, then I'd like to invite you to apply with me personally. You can apply here: **bit.ly/cbgdoneforyou**

After you've applied, a member of my team will give you a call and explain the program and see if it's a good fit for you. If it is, then we could actually be on a call in the next few days and sitting around a table together in the near future.

Thank you so much for taking the time to read this book and I hope we have the opportunity to meet in the near future.

Testimonials

Thank you Nick For a fabulous training day last week. I am so excited about putting lots of your ideas into practice. Your advice and expertise is in the back of my mind in all that I do now. I have shared lots already with my leadership team, we are well on the way to creating our VIP members cards and I have deliveries of mince pies planned for Christmas. I am trying to find ways to add a "call to action" on all that we do too. Very excited about the future.

Nick came to lead a training event with us recently. The day was absolutely jam packed with so many ideas not only to market our Nursery but to ensure our VIP's (and other local businesses) are raving about us and doing our marketing for us. Nick makes the training fun, engaging and relevant to all aspects of owning a Nursery. It was the most informative and motivating course I've been on since starting our Nursery. I am finally inspired to work ON my business rather than just enjoying the time IN it. THANK YOU!!!!

Claire Dancer

 Nick thank you so much for taking the time to come down to Buckfastleigh yesterday and supporting our little group of Nursery Owners and inspiring us with all of your amazing and thought-provoking ideas to market our nurseries. I was buzzing on the drive ho,e and this morning when my team arrived we spent two hours just chatting and going through a tiny portion of the ideas you shared with us yesterday. I've not actually had a chance to properly read your amazing book yet because my staff have each been reading it in turn whilst on their lunch breaks and then coming down and chatting with their teams about ideas and tips they have read about in your book. Sooooooo hopefully I will get a chance to read it this evening.

I would highly recommend any Nursery Owner, Preschool Leader or Childminder with Assistants attending this course it is pretty amazing and although a little more expensive than training I have attended in the past for Marketing put on by my local authority it is without doubt 1000% better and I will be using lots of your ideas and tips, so thank you. What was soooooo impressive was that you were clearly speaking from experience both with your knowledge of marketing and your more recent knowledge as a Nursery owner, so thank you.

Denise Tupman

Thank you Nick For a fabulous training day last week. I am so excited about putting lots of your ideas into practice. Your advice and expertise is in the back of my mind in all that I do now. I have shared lots already with my leadership team, we are well on the way to creating our VIP members cards and I have deliveries of mince pies planned for Christmas. I am trying to find ways to add a "call to action" on all that we do too. Very excited about the future.

Tricia Wellings

What a fantastic read! This book is essential to everyone in early years. No matter how good you think your marketing is, there will be something in this book that you won't have thought of. It's the little touches that make the customer feel wanted and appreciated that really ice the cake. As managers and owners it is one thing coming up with marketing strategies at the top but it is really the staff at the face of the work who sell the places and build those connections. Thank you Nick for the inspiration.

Mikey Boulden

Thoroughly enjoyed the course at the weekend. Found it really useful. Am going to use the tips for all the settings that I am Marketing Manager for. My aim is to increase our Occupancy levels using all of Nick's training tips and idea.

Nicola Taylor

Buzzing/ head full of ideas/ loads of exciting things to focus on/ loads of ideas/ really motivated- just some of the comments from my Mastermind group following the training from Nick yesterday! Thank you so very much Nick- we all had a great day and have come away with so many good ideas (just need to put them into place now- but some of us have already started!!) Highly recommend Nick's training- pitched at just the right level, interactive and full of exciting ideas and suggestions. Thanks Nick!

Katie Porter

Thank you so much Nick Williams for your visit to my nursery yesterday. Your tips, advice, and knowledge of marketing were very inspirational. My team really enjoyed talking to you about their role in the setting, and what they love about it. The testimonials you received from parents really boosted my confidence, and proved to me how good we are. I'm really looking forward to more discussion with you in the future. I highly recommend anyone looking for help and advice with their childcare marketing to get in touch with Nick. Thanks again for your time and support.

Denise 'Lady of Glencoe' Phelps

Lightning Source UK Ltd.
Milton Keynes UK
UKHW021958040520
362762UK00004B/7